“Bedtime reading just got a lot cooler and more spiritual. *Scripture Princesses* is perfect for any parent who wants the scriptures to come alive for their daughters. A must-read for your collection!”

—Benjamin Hyrum White, author of *I Hope They Call Me on a Mission, 10 Questions to Answer While Preparing for a Mission,* and *10 Questions to Answer After Serving a Mission*

“*Scripture Princesses* is a treasure to read. Greenwood testifies through illustration and text of the divine roles women have in God’s kingdom. She retells histories of women’s virtues in a clear and concise manner to motivate every young reader to be a force for good. This book is a valuable addition to any home library.”

—Annalisa Hall, bestselling author and author of *The Holy Ghost Is like a Blanket* and *I Want to Be Baptized*

“With so many worldly role models vying for our children’s attention, it is refreshing to see a book filled with examples of strong, faithful, and inspiring women. With a wide assortment of women from the scriptures, *Scripture Princesses* highlights women from the Old Testament, the New Testament, the Book of Mormon, and even the Doctrine and Covenants. Each story is presented in a way that is engaging and interesting to young readers and gives youth a wonderful introduction to the women of the scriptures. Rebecca Greenwood has done a fantastic job sharing these women’s stories, and this book is one that is sure to inspire young women for many years to come!”

—Heather Farrell, author of *Walking with the Women of the New Testament* and www.womeninthescriptures.com

"I love this book! *Scripture Princesses* spotlights the many inspiring, smart, and spiritual women of the scriptures and gives suggestions for how we can become more like each one of them. Readers young and old will find a new appreciation for these remarkable heroines and will likely learn details they never knew before. Greenwood's narrative style, dialogue, and detail work together to bring the scriptures to life. This is a book I highly recommend for anyone looking for a new approach to studying our treasured scripture stories."

—Heidi Poelman, author of *A is for Abinadi*
and *A Mother's Greatest Gift*

Scripture Princesses

Stories of Righteous Daughters of God

Written and Illustrated by

Rebecca J. Greenwood

CFI
An Imprint of Cedar Fort, Inc.
Springville, Utah

This is not an official publication of The Church of Jesus Christ of Latter-day Saints. The opinions and views expressed herein belong solely to the authors and do not necessarily represent the opinions or views of Cedar Fort, Inc. Permission for the use of sources, graphics, and photos is also solely the responsibility of the authors.

ISBN 13: 978-1-4621-1653-9

Published by CFI, an imprint of Cedar Fort, Inc.
2373 W. 700 S., Springville, UT 84663
Distributed by Cedar Fort, Inc., www.cedarfort.com

LIBRARY OF CONGRESS CATALOGING-IN-PUBLICATION DATA

Greenwood, Rebecca J., 1980- author.
Scripture princesses / Rebecca J. Greenwood.
pages cm
Includes bibliographical references and index.
ISBN 978-1-4621-1653-9 (alk. paper)
1. Women in the Bible--Biography. 2. Mormon women--Biography. I. Title.

BS575.G744 2015
220.9'2082--dc23

2015014816

Cover design by Shawnda T. Craig
Cover design © 2015 Lyle Mortimer
Edited and typeset by Jessica B. Ellingson

Printed in the United States of America

10 9 8 7 6 5 4 3 2 1

Printed on acid-free paper

For my nieces: Kira, Emma, Rachel, Juliet,
Brianna, Naomi, Abigail, and Daphne.

And for my future daughters.

Contents

Introduction

You are a daughter of God, a princess, sent to earth to learn and grow. You want to live your life well so that you can go back to Heavenly Father and be crowned with glory, like a queen.

This life is a test to see if we will choose to follow Heavenly Father when we don't have to. If we do choose to follow Him, Heavenly Father has promised us crowns of glory (see D&C 109:76).

The scriptures are full of stories of Heavenly Father's children choosing to follow Him and the great things they were able to do when they did. The lives of the great men and women of the scriptures were written down so we could use them as models of how we should live our lives. The scriptures contain the stories we can build our lives on.

But often when I read the scriptures, it feels like there are few women. Where are the girls I can model my life on—the women to be my heroines?

The women are there, though sometimes few are named. In this book, I have focused on sixteen of these heroic women from the scriptures. We have their names and the details of the great things they did in their lives.

These princesses of God from the earth's history had faith through hard trials. They faced things we may face in our lives. They lived God's law through difficulties like

- government oppression (Miriam, Esther)
- infertility or childlessness (Sarah, Rebekah, Rachel, Hannah, Elisabeth)
- poverty (Ruth and Naomi, Mary, Lucy, Emma)
- being uprooted from their homes (Sarah, Sariah, Mary, Emma)
- losing loved ones in death (Mary and Martha, Mary Magdalene, Emma)
- being alone in their faith (Abish)
- persecution from wicked men (Emma)
- loved ones falling away from God (Sariah)

They were also able to accomplish great things and see wonderful blessings come into their lives as they followed God's commandments despite the hard trials they faced.

Sometimes they made mistakes. These were real women, dealing with life. As they continued to strive to be like God, Jesus Christ's Atonement made up for their mistakes, and a legacy of good is the result.

Through their examples, we too can overcome and accomplish all the great things Heavenly Father wants us to accomplish in our mortal test. As we follow Heavenly Father and Jesus Christ, you and I can succeed in our princess test. We can build up God's kingdom and, with the help of Christ's Atonement, come back to live with God, crowned as royal heirs with Christ.

Notes

In these stories, I have tried to keep things close to the scriptural account while also, when I could, keeping events in the points of view of the women themselves. I also included connected stories of other women that are in the scriptural record, like the Hebrew midwives Puah and Shiphrah and the daughters of Onitah recorded in Abraham. I think these stories are important, and the contributions and sacrifices of these daughters of God should be recognized. They are women who faced down kings and daughters who chose death rather than betray their God.

In the illustrations, I have strived for accuracy while also allowing myself freedom to interpret. I scoured the Internet for resources on what these women in their cultures and time periods might have actually worn. I used photos of Bedouin women from the turn of the twentieth century and worked to figure out actual Achaemenid Persian fashion for Esther. The beehive dome houses of Harran, Turkey, are probably a thousand years out of period for Rebekah, Rachel, and Leah, but that architecture was too fun not to include. Also, the members of the Lamanite court of Lamoni likely weren't wearing classical Mayan fashion with a mix of current traditional Guatemalan Mayan clothing, but their clothes and culture are exciting and beautiful, so I decided to use them as my Lamanite models.

It was also interesting and frustrating to realize that in most cultures around the world, having an uncovered head was actually a more remarkable thing than having a covered one. It is only in our time of cars and air conditioning that hats have gone out of constant use. So I've struggled to keep faces clear through all the headscarves, wraps, and bonnets.

I hope the art and stories of this book will help bring the lives of these remarkable women alive for you.

Chapter 1

Eve

Be wise, like Eve

LONG, LONG ago, God and Christ worked together to create the world. They planned and created all things spiritually before they made them physically.

They created Adam and Eve, our first parents. They made Adam and Eve's bodies in the same form and image as God's body.

God created Adam first. He put him in the Garden of Eden and asked him to take care of it.

Adam was alone. God said to Jesus, "It is not good for man to be alone. I will make a companion for him." So He made beautiful Eve.

Adam and Eve were to take care of all the earth and all the animals. God brought all the animals to Adam as they were created, and Adam gave them names.

God commanded Adam and Eve to have children—to be fruitful and multiply.

He also told them they could eat fruit from all of the trees growing in the Garden of Eden, except for one. They were not to eat fruit from the tree of knowledge of good and evil. If they did, they would have to leave the garden, and they would die. The Lord said they could choose for themselves. "But remember, I forbid it."

Adam and Eve lived together in the garden. They tended it and ate the fruit that grew there. They were naked and innocent.

But they didn't have any joy or happiness because they never felt pain or misery. They didn't do any evil, but they didn't do any good either. They stayed there, in an unchanging state, unable to have children.

One day, Satan came to the garden. He had been cast out from God's presence because he wanted to deny mankind choices, and because he wanted to take God's power. He didn't understand God's plan. He wanted to destroy the world.

He pretended he was a snake. Satan talked to Eve. "Has God actually said that you shouldn't eat from every tree in the garden?"

Eve answered, "We may eat from all the trees, except from that one, in the middle of the garden. God said we shouldn't eat from it, or even touch it, or we will die."

"You won't die," said the serpent. "God knows it will cause your eyes to be opened. You will be like the gods, knowing good and evil."

Eve considered the beautiful tree. The fruit looked delicious, and she wanted the wisdom and knowledge the serpent said it would give her. She knew things needed to change. So she ate the fruit.

She brought the fruit to Adam and convinced him to eat it.

Their eyes opened, and they saw things as they hadn't before. They realized they were naked. They sewed fig leaves together to make aprons to cover themselves.

As they were walking in the garden in the cool evening, they heard the voice of the Lord. Adam and Eve hid from God in the trees of the garden.

"Adam, where are you going?" asked the Lord.

Adam answered, "I heard your voice and I was afraid, because I was naked. So I hid."

"Who told you that you were naked? Have you eaten from the tree I commanded you not to eat from?"

"Eve ate the fruit and gave some to me. I ate it to stay with her."

The Lord asked Eve why she had done this. She answered, "The snake tricked me, and I ate the fruit."

Because Adam and Eve had chosen to eat the fruit, God put the curse of mortality on them and on the whole world. Adam and Eve would eventually die, and so would everything that was born on earth. "For your body is dust, and to dust it will return."

God cursed the ground. It would now take work to grow food. Eve would be able to have children, but it would be painful for her. They would have to work together to feed their family.

The Lord made clothing of animal skins for them to wear.

Adam and Eve could now tell good from evil. They could also sin.

There was another tree in the garden—the tree of life. If Adam and Eve ate the fruit from that tree now, they would live forever, but in a sinful state. They would never be able to be in God's presence again.

To prevent this, the Lord drove Adam and Eve out of the garden and placed angels with a flaming sword in front of the tree of life to guard it.

Adam and Eve went out into the world. It was hard, but they worked together. They farmed, tilled the earth, and took care of animals. They followed the Lord's commandments. Adam and Eve loved each other.

Eve bore children—sons and daughters. She and Adam loved their children.

Adam and Eve prayed to God, and He spoke to them from the direction of the Garden of Eden, but they didn't see Him anymore. They were shut out of His presence.

The Lord commanded them to offer sacrifices of the firstborn animals from their flocks. The sacrifices represented the sacrifice God's Son, Jesus Christ, would make to atone for Adam's fall and for the sins all of mankind would commit.

Adam praised God. "Because I ate the fruit, my eyes are opened. In this life I will have joy, and in my flesh I will see God.

Eve was glad as well. "If we had not eaten the fruit, we would never have had children. We wouldn't have known good and evil, or the joy of our redemption and the eternal life that God will give to all the obedient."

Eve was so happy she was able to have her children. She realized that their fall was worth the hardship. By learning good from evil and experiencing pain and unhappiness, she was able to become wise and have joy. She knew that if they did well in this fallen life, they would be much happier than they were ever able to be in the perfect but unchanging garden.

Adam and Eve praised God and taught all these things to their children.

Read Eve's story in

Genesis 1–4 Moses 2–5 2 Nephi 2:17–27

Chapter 2

Sarah

Be faithful, like Sarah

LONG, LONG ago, in the city of Ur in Mesopotamia, Sarai lived with her family. The people of the city were wicked and had turned from worshipping God to worshipping idols—false gods they had made up. They murdered their own children, killing them as sacrifices to the false gods.

Sarai's close relative Abram was a righteous man who believed in God and had sought to be ordained to the true priesthood. He visited the great high priest Melchizedek and was ordained. His father, Terah, however, worshipped the false idols with the people of their city. He was unhappy with his son because Abram refused to worship the idols. Terah conspired with the evil priests to sacrifice his son to the idols.

Abram was captured and taken to be sacrificed. With him were three princesses from the line of Ham, the daughters of Onitah. These sisters were righteous and had also refused to worship the false gods. The evil priests killed the sisters on the altar in front of the idols.

God let the priests kill the righteous sisters. God has given all of us agency, the ability to choose between good and evil. The priests chose evil and murder. God allows people to choose to do evil so He can be just in punishing them.

The evil priests tied Abram to the altar and were about to sacrifice him as well. An angel from God came down and saved Abram. The angel destroyed the evil priest, the altar, and the idols.

Abram and Sarai got married and left the wicked city Ur, taking Abram's nephew Lot with them.

There was a famine in all the land, and little food and water was available for the people. Abram's father, Terah, followed them out of the city. They lived together for many years in Haran.

But eventually, Terah went back to worshipping idols. God told Abram and Sarai to leave their father and relatives and get out. They took Lot and all those who had been converted to the Lord with them.

They became nomads, wandering in the wilderness of the Middle East and living in tents. It was still hard to find food, so they headed to the rich land of Egypt.

Sarai was a beautiful woman. God told Abram and Sarai that the Egyptians would kill Abram because they wanted his beautiful wife. To prevent that, they were to tell the Egyptians that she was his sister.

In Egypt, the Egyptian princes saw Sarai's beauty and brought her to the attention of Pharaoh. Pharaoh decided he wanted her as one of his wives and took her into his house. He gave Abram gifts of riches and servants in exchange for his "sister."

A plague immediately fell upon Pharaoh's house.

Pharaoh called in Abram, demanding to know why these things were happening. Abram said that Sarai was really his wife. Pharaoh gave her back to Abram, and the plague immediately stopped.

Because of this, Pharaoh listened to Abram. He was able to teach Pharaoh and his court about astronomy.

When Abram and Sarai left Egypt, they left with riches, flocks, herds, and servants. They returned to the land of Canaan.

Abram and Sarai grew old, but they still did not have any children. They wished and prayed for children more than anything else, and the Lord had promised them that they would have children. But still, years passed without Sarai becoming pregnant.

When Abram was ninety-nine years old, the Lord made a covenant with him and changed his name to Abraham, which means "a father of many nations." The Lord changed Sarai's name to Sarah, which means "princess."

God assured Abraham that Sarah would have a child. Abraham laughed for joy that Sarah would have a baby.

A little later, three holy men came to visit Abraham. He was happy to see them, and he asked Sarah to make bread and a servant to prepare meat for them.

They sat under a tree and ate. The men spoke together, and one said that Sarah would have a baby. Sarah was at the tent door and overheard. She laughed in disbelief. She was ninety years old, and her body was past the age to have a baby.

The holy man asked why Sarah laughed. Startled that they had heard her, she denied laughing. The holy man said, "Nothing is too hard for the Lord."

Sarah had remained righteous and obedient to God through the many long years of her life. She knew God had promised she would have children, and she waited on the Lord to fulfill His promises with faith. She finally did become pregnant, and she had a baby boy. They named him Isaac, which means "laughter," because they laughed for joy to be able to have a child in their old age.

The Lord blessed Abraham and Sarah because they were righteous, and as their grandchildren and great-grandchildren were born and time went on, they became the parents of millions—the tribes of Israel, the Jews, and Jesus Christ.

As part of God's covenant with Abraham, all those who are baptized into the gospel of Christ are adopted into Abraham's lineage. And so, all righteous followers of Christ are also the children of Abraham and Sarah.

Read Sarah's story in

Abraham 1–2 Genesis 11–23

Chapter 3

Rebekah

Be kind, like Rebekah

LONG, LONG ago in the land of Canaan, Isaac's mother, Sarah, died. He and his father, Abraham, mourned for her.

Abraham didn't want Isaac to marry any of the women from the land where they were living because they didn't worship God. They had other religions with multiple gods. Abraham knew his relatives in the distant land of Haran worshipped the Lord, but he didn't want to send Isaac, the only child Sarah had borne, to this distant land by himself. The Lord had commanded Abraham to leave his father and his relatives, so Abraham didn't intend to go there himself.

So Abraham called in his chief servant and commanded him to go to the land of Haran, find a wife for Isaac, and bring her back with him.

The servant was worried. Why would a woman come with him and leave her family to marry a man she had never met?

Abraham assured him that the Lord would direct him and help him find a wife for Isaac, a woman of faith who would agree to come.

The servant took ten camels and his men and traveled to Mesopotamia, to the city of Nahor, named for Abraham's brother. When he got there, he had his camels kneel by the well outside the city. It was evening, and the women of the city were coming to the well to draw water for their families.

The servant prayed to the Lord for help in finding the girl for Isaac. He prayed for a sign. He told the Lord that he would ask each girl at the well if he could have a drink from their water. If one of the girls gave him water to drink and also volunteered to water his camels, that girl would be the right girl for Isaac.

He approached a beautiful young girl and asked her, "Will you give me water from your pitcher?"

She said, "Yes!" She took her full pitcher off of her shoulder and poured water for him to drink.

She then said, "I'll draw water for your camels as well." She was kind to this stranger she had just met.

The servant was excited. The Lord had answered his prayer! Here was the right girl.

He gave her a gold ring and gold bracelets and asked her who she was.

"I am Rebekah, daughter of Bethuel, son of Milcah and Nahor."

She was a granddaughter of Abraham's brother. The servant rejoiced. He had found Isaac's wife-to-be, and she was from Abraham's extended family.

He told her he was a servant of Abraham, her grandfather's brother, and asked if he and his men could stay with her family that night.

She went to her mother and brother and told them about the servant. Her brother Laban ran and met the servant and invited him to stay with them.

Before they sat down to eat, the servant told them why he was there and how the Lord had answered his prayer and led him to Rebekah. He asked if he could take Rebekah to marry Abraham's son Isaac.

They said, "It looks like it is from the Lord, and the Lord has arranged it." They gave permission.

The servant gave Rebekah more jewelry and clothes as bridal gifts and gave gifts to her family as well.

The next morning, the servant wanted to leave for Canaan immediately.

Rebekah's family wanted her to leave a little later. "Give her at least ten days."

But the servant insisted. The Lord had answered his prayer, and he didn't want to wait any longer.

They said, "Well then, let Rebekah decide."

They called her in.

"Are you willing to go with this man?"

She said, "I will go."

So she went with him, taking her nurse and some maidservants.

As they were leaving, her mother and brother said to her, "May you be the mother of thousands of millions."

Isaac was in the fields alone, meditating, when he saw the caravan of camels returning. He went to meet them.

Rebekah saw a man approaching. She dismounted from her camel and asked the servant, "Who is this man coming over to us?"

"That is our master."

When she realized it was Isaac, who was to be her husband, she took her veil and covered her face.

They were married, and Isaac took her into the tent that had been his mother's, and she comforted him in his mourning.

Isaac loved her.

They lived together happily for many years but didn't have any children. After twenty long years, she finally became pregnant.

It was a hard pregnancy, with the baby kicking and jostling in her womb.

She prayed to the Lord and asked what was going on.

He answered and said, "Two nations are in your womb, and two types of people. One shall be stronger than the other, and the elder will serve the younger."

When she delivered, she had twins! The older was red-haired Esau, who became a hunter, and the younger was Jacob, who liked to live more quietly.

When they were older, Esau sold his birthright, his rights as the eldest son, to Jacob. Rebekah helped Jacob get the birthright blessing from his father to fulfill the prophecy of the Lord that had been given to her before they were born. Jacob would become Israel and be father to the twelve tribes of Israel.

Rebekah lived a long life of service to God and her family. She was kind and quick to act when she knew it was something God wanted her to do.

Read Rebekah's story in

Genesis 24–27

Chapter 4

Rachel & Leah

Marry in the covenant, like Rachel and Leah

LONG, LONG ago in the city of Haran, Laban, the brother of Rebekah, had two daughters, Leah and Rachel. Rachel was beautiful and popular, but Leah was considered "tender-eyed."

Rachel took care of her father's flocks of sheep. One day, as she was taking the sheep to the well to draw water for them, a handsome stranger was there, talking to the other people of the town. The townspeople had told the man who she was. When he saw her, he rolled the stone away from the top of the well for her, and then came up to her and kissed her!

He cried out with joy and wept and let her know that he was her cousin, the son of her aunt Rebekah. His name was Jacob.

Rachel ran and told her father, Laban. He invited Jacob to stay with them.

Jacob told them he had left his parents because his twin brother, Esau, was angry with him and wanted to kill him. His mother, Rebekah, had sent him to Haran to be safe and find a good wife from her brother's people who believed in God. Jacob wanted to marry a girl who was from the covenant line. He knew he could find one like that in his mother's family.

After Jacob had stayed with them for a month, helping them with their work, Laban asked him what wages he'd like in exchange for the work he had been doing for them.

Jacob said that he loved Rachel. "I will serve you seven years so that I can marry your daughter."

Laban agreed to the bargain.

Jacob worked for Laban for seven years. He loved Rachel so much that he considered those years like one day.

But Rachel's older sister, Leah, was still unmarried. Laban didn't like this. So he tricked Jacob. For the wedding, Laban disguised Leah with a heavy veil. The next morning, Jacob discovered he had married the wrong sister! It was Leah with him.

Jacob went to Laban, angrily demanding an explanation. "I worked for you so I could marry Rachel!"

Laban excused himself, saying, "In our country, the younger sister does not get married before the older. Give Leah a week as your wife, and I will give you Rachel to marry as well. But you will need to work seven more years for me."

Jacob had little choice but to agree, and after a week, he and Rachel were finally able to marry. Jacob now had two wives, but he loved Rachel more than he loved Leah.

Leah was fertile and had children easily, but Rachel was not.

Leah was unhappy that her husband did not love her as much. She bore four sons, and with each one, she hoped Jacob would love her more.

Rachel was loved, but she was not having children, and her sister was. She was so unhappy. She wanted babies as well.

She went to Jacob and said, "Give me children, or I will die!"

Jacob was angry back. "It's up to the Lord. I can't do anything about it."

Rachel decided to give Jacob her maidservant Bilhah to be a wife for him, and Bilhah would have children for her.

Bilhah had two sons. When Leah saw she had slowed in becoming pregnant, she gave her maidservant Zilpah to Jacob to be his fourth wife and have children for her as well. This servant also had two sons. Then Leah had a few more sons. In the end, Leah had six sons and one daughter for Jacob. And Rachel still had none.

At last, God blessed Rachel. She became pregnant and had a son. She called him Joseph.

After all this time away from home, about twenty years, the Lord told Jacob he needed to go back to Canaan, where his parents and brother lived. He talked to his wives, and they told him, "What God has told you to do, do."

Rachel and Leah were willing to leave their father and home and go into foreign lands with their husband and children. In his time with Laban, Jacob and his family had become rich with livestock and servants.

When Jacob met with his brother Esau again, Esau was no longer angry with him. He was glad to see his twin.

Rachel did have one more son, Benjamin. But she died in childbirth and was unable to raise him.

Rachel and Leah struggled, but they worked hard and loved their family. They married in the covenant, obeyed the Lord, and were faithful.

In the end, Jacob had twelve sons. The Lord changed Jacob's name to Israel. The children of his sons became the twelve tribes of Israel, who carried on the covenant God had given to Abraham.

Rachel's son Joseph was sold by his jealous brothers into Egypt, and eventually Joseph was able to prepare a way for his large family to move to Egypt during a terrible famine. He saved his family members' lives.

Jacob's family and posterity settled in Egypt until they were led out by Moses many years later.

Read Rachel & Leah's story in

Genesis 29–33

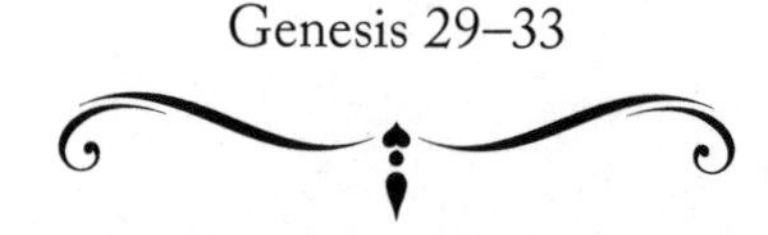

Chapter 5

Miriam

Be bold, like Miriam

LONG, LONG ago, in the land of Egypt, the children of Israel, called the Hebrews, were becoming numerous, strong, and mighty. As the years passed, the people of Egypt became nervous and wary of them, thinking that they might become more powerful than they were. To keep the Hebrews from becoming stronger than the native Egyptians, the Egyptians made them into slaves. They put heavy burdens on their backs and kept tight control over them. But the Hebrews got even stronger and continued to have more children.

So Pharaoh, the king of Egypt, sent for the midwives of the Hebrew people, Shiphrah and Puah. Pharaoh commanded them that whenever a Hebrew woman birthed a male baby, the midwives were to kill the baby.

Shiphrah and Puah obeyed God before they would obey Pharaoh. They didn't kill the baby boys. Pharaoh noticed and called them in again, "Why are you not obeying me?"

The midwives told him, "Hebrew women are faster than Egyptian women. They are delivering their babies before we even get there."

Because the midwives protected the Hebrew children, God blessed them. But Pharaoh was determined. He sent out an order to his own people. Whenever there was a baby boy born to a Hebrew woman, the Egyptians were to throw the baby into the Nile River.

Miriam was a Hebrew girl who lived with her parents and brother, Aaron, as a slave in Egypt. Her mother, Jochebed, had a baby boy and hid him for three months, until she couldn't hide him any longer.

Jochebed made a basket of river reeds into an ark with a lid and waterproofed it with mud and pitch, or tar. She put her baby

in the ark and laid it in the reeds on the edge of the river Nile. She put her baby in the river, as Pharaoh commanded.

She asked Miriam to watch from a distance, to see what would happen to her little brother in the ark.

The daughter of Pharaoh, a princess of Egypt, came down to the river to bathe. Her maidservants, walking along the edge of the Nile, saw the ark in the reeds. The princess told her servants to get it and bring it to her. They pulled the basket out of the water and presented it to the princess. She opened the lid and discovered the baby. The baby started to cry.

"This is one of the Hebrew children," the princess said. She felt sorry for the baby and decided to adopt him.

Miriam saw all this, and she boldly came up to the princess and said, "Shall I go and find a wet nurse for the baby from the Hebrew people? She could nurse the baby for you."

The princess agreed. Miriam went and brought her mother to the princess. The princess gave the baby to Jochebed and paid her to nurse the baby until he was weaned.

Then Miriam's mother brought the baby boy to the princess. She decided to call him Moses. Miriam's brother Moses was raised as a prince in Egypt in the princess's household.

Years later, after he was grown, Moses became a prophet. He was led by the Lord and was able to free his people from slavery. Miriam and Aaron helped him lead the Hebrews out of Egypt.

Miriam was considered a prophetess and leader among the Hebrew women. As they left Egypt, she led the women in a song and dance, singing, "Sing ye to the Lord!"

Miriam's boldness saved her brother's life and helped lead to her people being freed from slavery.

Read Miriam's story in

Exodus 1–2; 15:20–21

Chapter 6

Ruth & Naomi

Be loyal, like Ruth

LONG, LONG ago, in the town of Bethlehem in Israel, Naomi lived with her husband and two sons. There was a famine in the land, and they didn't have any food. Naomi and her family moved to Moab, which is a country next to Israel, where there was food. They lived in Moab for several years. Then Naomi's husband died. Her two sons married Orpah and Ruth, women from the town they were living in. They lived there happily for ten years, though neither of the sons and their wives had any children in those years. Then, unexpectedly, Naomi's two sons also died. All who were left were Naomi and her two daughters-in-law.

Part of the Mosaic Law outlined by Jehovah was that if a brother died without any children, the next brother should marry

his brother's widow, and have their children be in the name of his brother, to inherit all the brother's land and status. However, Naomi didn't have any more sons. She had nothing to offer her daughters-in-law anymore.

Naomi heard there was no longer a famine in Israel, so she decided to go back home.

She told her daughters-in-law, "Go home to your families here in Moab. I'm going to go back to my own land." Orpah and Ruth loved Naomi, and they cried together.

Orpah decided she would go back to her own family, but Ruth hugged Naomi and said, "Please don't ask me to leave you. Where you go, I will go, and where you stay, I will stay. Your people will be my people, and your God will be my God."

The people of Moab didn't believe in the God of Israel. Ruth had a different religion. But she decided to become a faithful Jew and live with Naomi as her daughter. She loved Naomi and was loyal to her. So they moved to Israel, two poor widows, with only themselves to help each other.

When harvest time came in Israel, poor people were allowed to glean in the fields. As workers went through a field and harvested the grain, they were not to pick up anything that dropped out of

their bundles, but instead they left it on the ground. Poor people would travel behind, picking up whatever grain was left on the ground. This was called gleaning.

Naomi sent Ruth to glean in the fields at harvest time so they could have barley and wheat for bread through the winter. Ruth went to a field where people were harvesting and started to glean.

The owner of the field where Ruth was gleaning noticed her and asked his people around him, "Who is this woman? I don't know her."

"This is Naomi's daughter-in-law Ruth from Moab, who has left her own land to help Naomi."

The landowner's name was Boaz, a close relative of Naomi's dead husband, and he admired Ruth for all she was doing to help Naomi and for her loyalty.

He went up to her and said, "You stay in my fields and glean here. Stay close to my women workers."

He instructed his workers to leave extra on the ground for her so Ruth and Naomi would have enough to eat.

When Ruth got home that night, she came with a lot of grain and told Naomi what had happened. Naomi was excited that her dead husband's relative had shown kindness and admiration to Ruth. Naomi saw a possible opportunity.

Through the harvest, Boaz continued to show kindness to Ruth, and even fed her with his workers.

Naomi decided to try something. She hoped to ask him to marry Ruth like one of her sons would have done, to take care of the two widows, and have children for her dead husband's line.

Naomi gave Ruth specific instructions on what to do, for she was from a different country and didn't know all the cultural practices of Israel. She was to go and uncover Boaz's feet in the night, lie down at his feet, and ask him to "cover her with his skirt," or protect her and marry her.

Ruth bravely did as Naomi instructed. She went to where Boaz was sleeping on the threshing floor, guarding his harvest. She uncovered his feet and lay down. He did not wake up until midnight, and when he did, he was startled to find someone lying there at his feet.

She told him, "I am Ruth." And she asked him to marry her! "Because you are a close relative," she explained.

Boaz admired her even more and said, "Well, I could. But there is one man who is a closer relative than I am. I will ask him first if he will marry you. If he will not, I will."

He sent her back home quietly, so no one would know she had been there. He filled her headscarf with grain to take back home with her.

The next morning, Boaz went into town and hailed the other close relative on the street. He called him over, as well as several other elders of the town, and had them sit down. Boaz asked the man, Ploni Almoni, if he wanted to buy the land that Naomi's family owned. "Sure," he said.

Then Boaz said, "If you buy this land, you will need to marry Ruth, Naomi's daughter-in-law."

Ploni was uninterested in marrying Ruth. So Boaz stated in front of the elders of the town that he was purchasing Naomi's land and was going to marry Ruth.

Once Boaz and Ruth were married, they had a son, Obed. Naomi lived with them and was so happy with her grandson.

Obed was grandfather to King David, and many generations later, Jesus Christ was born to King David's line.

Because of Ruth's loyalty to Naomi and to her new faith, she was blessed to be an ancestor of Jesus Christ.

Read Ruth & Naomi's story in
Ruth 1–4

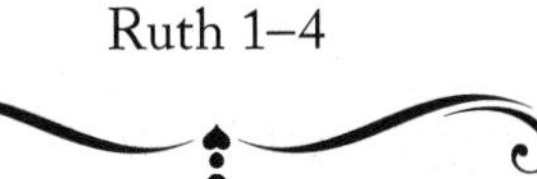

Chapter 7

Hannah

Be prayerful, like Hannah

Long, long ago, in Shiloh in the land of Israel, Hannah came every year with her husband and his household to offer sacrifices to the Lord at the tabernacle.

Hannah's husband was Elkanah. He had another wife, named Peninnah, who had several children. But Hannah had no children, which made her sad.

As Elkanah divided up the portions for their sacrifices, he gave a portion to Peninnah and to each of her children, but he gave an extra portion to Hannah because he loved her.

Peninnah mocked Hannah for her childlessness and was mean to her. She upset Hannah so much that at dinner that night, Hannah wept and refused to eat.

Elkanah came to his wife and asked her, “Why are you crying? Why won’t you eat? Why does your heart grieve? Am I not better to you than ten sons?”

Hannah’s soul still grieved. After dinner, she went to the tabernacle, which was their temple, and stood outside. She prayed to the Lord in her mind, moving her lips but not speaking out loud.

She made a promise to the Lord. “Oh, Lord of hosts, please look on the affliction of your handmaid, and remember me, and don’t forget me. If you will give me a son, I will give him to the Lord all the days of his life, and no razor shall come on his head.”

She vowed to the Lord that if He granted her a son, she would dedicate him to the Lord as a Nazarite. Nazarites were people who gave a special promise to the Lord and never cut their hair or drank wine.

Eli the priest sat in an official seat at the post of the tabernacle, and he saw Hannah there. He saw that her lips moved without speaking, and so he thought she was drunk.

He came up to her. "Stop drinking so much wine," he said.

"No, my lord. I'm not drunk," she told him. "I'm just a sad woman. I'm pouring out my soul to God because I am full of grief."

Eli said, "Go in peace. The God of Israel will grant what you have asked of Him."

Hannah thanked him and left, now full of hope. She was able to eat.

The next morning, they got up early and worshipped at the tabernacle, and then they returned to their home in Ramah.

Hannah became pregnant soon after, and she had a baby boy. She called him Samuel.

The next year, when Elkanah went back to Shiloh with his family for their yearly sacrifices, she stayed behind in Ramah with her baby.

"I won't go up until the baby is weaned. Then I'll bring him before the Lord, and he'll stay there forever."

Elkanah agreed, "Do what seems right to you."

After Hannah weaned Samuel, she took the toddler to the tabernacle, along with three bulls, flour, and wine as offerings. She brought her young son to Eli the priest.

"My lord, I am the woman that stood by you here, praying to God. I asked the Lord for this child, and He granted my petition. So I lend him to the Lord for as long as he lives."

Hannah prayed aloud a song of praise:

My heart rejoices in the Lord,
my horn is exalted in the Lord,
my mouth is enlarged over my enemies
Because I rejoice in thy salvation.
There is none holy as the Lord:
for there is none beside thee:
neither is there any rock like our God.

Hannah and Elkanah returned home to Ramah, and Samuel stayed with Eli. Samuel grew up serving the Lord in the tabernacle.

Every year, Hannah would make clothes for Samuel and bring them to him when her family came up for their sacrifices.

Eli blessed Elkanah and Hannah. “The Lord give more children to you because of this son you lent to the Lord.”

Hannah did have more children—three sons and two daughters.

Samuel grew up to be a great prophet and judge in Israel. He was the prophet who anointed Saul and David to be kings of Israel.

Hannah’s prayers to the Lord were answered and led to great things for Israel.

Read Hannah’s story in

1 Samuel 1–2

Chapter 8

Sariah

Follow the prophet, like Sariah

LONG, LONG ago, in the city of Jerusalem, Sariah lived with her husband, Lehi, and her four sons, Laman, Lemuel, Sam, and Nephi—the youngest.

Lehi was a wealthy man who owned gold, silver, and land. He was also a prophet who was close to God. God sent him visions and dreams.

The city of Jerusalem had become wicked. God commanded Lehi to preach to the people and to tell them they must repent or the city would be destroyed. Lehi spoke out against the evil they were doing. The people of Jerusalem became angry with him and wanted to kill him.

God spoke to Lehi in a dream and told him to take his family, leave Jerusalem, and escape into the wilderness. In the morning, Lehi told Sariah, and she believed and trusted him. Lehi, Sariah, and their children gathered their tents and supplies and left the bulk of their wealth behind. They journeyed for several days in the wilderness and camped down by the Red Sea. Sariah left the comfort and security of her home to live in a tent because she believed her husband was a prophet of God.

After they had been there a few days, God commanded Lehi to send his sons back to Jerusalem and to return with the brass plates. Laban, a rich and powerful man in Jerusalem, owned the brass plates, upon which were written the scriptures. It was important that Lehi's family have a copy of the scriptures. So Lehi sent his sons to go and get them from Laban. Laman and Lemuel didn't want to go, but Nephi knew that if God commanded it, then they would be able to accomplish it. He led them back to the city.

Sariah knew Laban was not a good man and that this was a hard task. She feared for her sons. As the days passed and her sons still did not return, she began to fear that they had been killed.

Sariah was afraid. Her sons must be dead! She cried and mourned. She blamed her husband.

"My sons are no more! You have led us away from our home, and we will perish in the wilderness!"

Lehi tried to comfort her: "We would have been killed in Jerusalem if we had not left. We've obtained a land of promise from God. I know the Lord will deliver my sons out of the hands of Laban and bring them back."

Finally, the boys did return. It had been hard, but they had been successful in bringing back the brass plates, which held the writings of the prophets. They also brought one of Laban's servants, Zoram, with them. Nephi had to kill Laban to gain the plates, but he had been ordered by God to do it, and they had come back safely.

Sariah was comforted. She said, "Now I know for sure that the Lord has commanded us to do these things and that He will

help us accomplish them." She joined with Lehi in offering sacrifices and burnt offerings to give thanks to the Lord for protecting their sons.

After the miracle of her sons' protection and success, Sariah never again doubted the word of the Lord given through her husband, She supported him in everything.

Lehi read the brass plates and taught his family the words of the prophets from them. He prophesied these scriptures would be available to his descendants and that they would learn the words of the Lord from them.

A little later, God commanded again that Sariah's sons should be sent back to Jerusalem. They were to visit the family of Ishmael and convince them to leave with them. Her sons would be able to marry Ishmael's daughters. Sariah didn't mind this commandment from God and was happy when they came back with Ishmael, his wife, two of his sons and their wives, and his five daughters. They again offered burnt sacrifices to God in thanks.

As the two families started to work together, they gathered seeds for growing grains, fruits, and vegetables to take with them on their journey.

Lehi had a vivid and prophetic dream. He told his family that in the dream, an angel had shown him a beautiful tree with white fruit. Eating the fruit of the tree filled him with joy. In the dream, Sariah, Sam, and Nephi had joined Lehi in eating at the tree. Laman and Lemuel had refused.

There was a narrow path that led to the tree, and a rod of iron lined it. People who wanted to eat the tree's fruit had to hold onto the rod and walk the path through the darkness to reach the tree.

The tree was the tree of life. The rod was the word of God, which all should hold on to. And the fruit was the love of God.

Sariah's sons married the daughters of Ishmael. Zoram, the former servant of Laban, married Ishmael's eldest daughter. Nephi said he was exceedingly blessed in his marriage.

Sariah was now the matriarch of a large caravan, with daughters-in-law and Ishmael's wife to help, provide for, and work with. The women would be in charge of much of the cooking, cleaning, and caring for tents and animals as they traveled. They also supported each other as the women became pregnant and babies were born.

But there was conflict in this large group. Laman, Lemuel, their wives, and Ishmael's sons did not want to be there. They wanted to go back to Jerusalem. They didn't really believe Jerusalem was going to be destroyed. They didn't like traveling and the hardships of being in the wilderness away from civilization.

They resented how Nephi, the youngest, was most often the leader of the group under Lehi. Nephi received visions too and spoke forcefully to them about God's commandments.

Sariah's heart hurt every time her sons fought or were cruel to each other. The conflict between her eldest sons and their father and Nephi often became bad. They grumbled and muttered and complained. They had threatened to kill Nephi more than once.

The Lord spoke to Lehi in another dream and said they should start on their journey the next day. When they woke up, they found a strange ball outside Lehi and Sariah's tent door. It was like a compass made of fine brass. They called it the Liahona.

It worked according to the power of God. If they were faithful, it would point the way they should go. It would also occasionally give them messages from God. If they were not faithful, it would stop working completely.

While they traveled, the men of the company would hunt for food, but sometimes it was hard for them to find any.

They traveled for eight years. They had a lot of trials and afflictions in the wilderness.

All the women bore children while they traveled. Sariah had two more sons, Jacob and Joseph. At some point, she also had daughters.

The Lord told them not to use much fire in their camps. Instead, they ate their meat raw. The Lord told them, "I will make it sweet. I will be your light in the wilderness. You will know that I lead you."

The Lord blessed them. The women became strong and able to handle the travel and the work they had to do and were able to provide plenty of milk for their babies. Their children grew up strong. The group began to bear the journey without complaining.

After eight years, they reached a land that was so fertile and full of food that they called it Bountiful. It was on the shores of the ocean. The Lord spoke to Nephi and told him to build a ship; their promised land was across the ocean. They followed the Lord's instructions and built a ship that would take them across the ocean.

They prepared provisions harvested from the land around them, including honey, to take with them on the trip. The Lord spoke to Lehi and told them to enter the ship and depart.

The wind drove the ship and blew them toward the promised land.

After many days on the ship, some of the men and women decided to have a party where they danced and sang, but they also became very rude. They insulted the Lord.

Nephi spoke sharply to them, telling them to stop or the Lord might strike them down. They got angry with Nephi. Laman, Lemuel, and the sons of Ishmael grabbed Nephi and roughly tied him up with ropes. They didn't want Nephi telling them what to do. Immediately the Liahona stopped working. They didn't know where to steer the ship. A storm came, and for four days it battered the ship.

Lehi told them to let Nephi go, but they threatened to hurt anyone who tried to help him. Nephi's wife and children pleaded for him and prayed for God's help, but the angry men refused to listen.

Lehi and Sariah were old, and they became sick with grief at their sons' actions. They lay in their bed and could barely move. Young Jacob and Joseph cried and needed their mother, but Sariah couldn't help them. She was close to dying. The ship rocked and heaved in the storm.

The men were afraid the storm would destroy the ship and they would drown, but they refused to let Nephi go. On the

fourth day, the storm became so bad, the ship was about to be swallowed by the sea. They were about to die. The only thing Laman, Lemuel, and the sons of Ishmael could do to stop it was to untie Nephi.

They finally let Nephi go.

Nephi took the Liahona in his hands, and it started working again. Nephi prayed, and the storm ceased. The sea became calm. Nephi, with his wrists swollen and bleeding from the ropes, steered the ship toward the promised land again. Sariah and Lehi were able to recover from their illness.

Finally, they landed. They had reached the promised land. They planted the seeds they had brought with them, and the seeds grew. They found many animals living wild in the land they could use.

Lehi prophesied that no one should come to this land of promise except those who were brought by the hand of the Lord.

Sariah had obeyed the words of the prophet, her husband, Lehi. She had supported him in the wilderness. They now had a wonderful land of promise to live in. Her children prospered in this rich new land. They eventually divided into Nephites, who followed the Lord, and Lamanites, who didn't. Sariah's children grew into two great civilizations that warred against each other for a thousand years. The Savior would visit them, and the line of prophets coming from her lineage would write the Book of Mormon, which contains the fulness of the gospel.

Read Sariah's story in

1 Nephi 1–18 2 Nephi 1–5

Chapter 9

Queen Esther

Be brave, like Esther

LONG, LONG ago, in Shushan, the capital city of the ancient Persian Empire, lived a beautiful young woman named Esther, with her cousin Mordecai, who had raised her. They were Jews, but they lived in Persia because their family had been carried away from Jerusalem in a war.

The king of Persia, Ahasuerus, wanted a new queen. He commanded that beautiful young women from all the provinces of his empire should be brought to his palace, and he would choose a queen from among them.

Esther was chosen to be one of these maidens and was brought to live at the king's palace. She impressed everyone who met her there. She was given perfumes, spices, and myrrh to bathe in, seven maidservants to attend her, and the best room in the house of women at the palace.

Before Esther had left for the palace, Mordecai had warned her not to tell anyone that she was a Jew, or who her relatives were, in case this would put her in danger. So in the palace, no one knew she was Jewish.

Every day, Mordecai would walk by the court of the women's house to check how Esther was.

Esther lived in the palace for a year before it was her turn to go visit the king. When the king met Esther, he loved her above all the other women. He set the royal crown on her head and made her his queen.

Mordecai often sat at the king's gate. One day, he discovered that two of the keepers of the gate, servants of the king, were conspiring together to kill King Ahasuerus. Mordecai warned Esther, who warned the king, and the evil men were caught. The king's scribes wrote in the court's records that Mordecai had saved the king.

Around this time, the king promoted a man named Haman to be the chief prince over all the other princes in the land and commanded that all the king's servants should bow and reverence Haman. Mordecai, however, refused to bow to Haman.

The king's servants asked Mordecai, "Why do you disobey the king's commands?"

Mordecai told them that he was a Jew. He didn't believe in bowing down, except to God.

The king's servants told Haman how Mordecai refused to bow to him. Haman was angry that the Jew Mordecai did not bow and reverence him as he had been commanded. Haman wanted to kill Mordecai and decided he wanted to destroy all Jews as well.

Haman went to the king and told him, "There is a certain people scattered throughout all your provinces that follow different laws than all other people. They don't keep your laws. Let it be written that they are to be destroyed. I will pay ten thousand talents of silver to the king's treasury to see that it is done."

King Ahasuerus gave Haman his ring and permission to do it. Letters were sent to all the king's provinces, commanding the king's people to kill all the Jews, young and old, men, women, and children, in one day. Haman drew lots and chose the thirteenth day of the twelfth month Adar, which is in early March. Those who killed the Jews could take the Jews' belongings for themselves.

The king and Haman sat down with satisfaction, but everyone in the city of Shushan was perplexed at these orders.

When Mordecai saw this pronouncement, he tore his clothes, put on sackcloth, and poured ashes on his head. He cried in mourning in the city and outside the king's gate.

As the decree spread through the empire, the Jews in every province wept and wailed, fasted and prayed.

Esther in the palace heard that Mordecai was wearing sackcloth but didn't know why. She sent her chamberlain Hatach to him with new clothes, but Mordecai refused them. He told Hatach the king's decree and sent a copy to Esther.

Mordecai also sent a charge to Esther to go to the king, plead for their lives, and ask him not to allow this. Esther told Hatach to tell Mordecai, "There is a law that if anyone goes to the inner court of the king without being called by him, they are put to death unless the king puts out his scepter and accepts them. The king hasn't called for me to visit him for thirty days."

Mordecai sent his answer: "Don't think that you will escape this because you are in the palace. If you do not act, our deliverance will come from another place, but you will be destroyed. And perhaps you are in the place you are so that you can save your people."

Esther asked Mordecai to gather all the Jews that lived in Shushan and to fast for her for three days and three nights. "I and my maidens will fast as well. I will disobey the law and go in unto the king. And if I perish, I perish."

On the third day of fasting, Esther put on her royal apparel and bravely went into the inner court while the king sat on his throne.

When King Ahasuerus saw Esther in the inner court, he held out his scepter to her. She came up to him and touched the top of his scepter. He accepted her presence.

“What is your request, Queen Esther?” the king asked. “I will grant it, even to half the kingdom.”

Esther said, “If it seems good to the king, I invite you and Haman to a feast that I have prepared today.”

The king called Haman to quickly come, and they went to the queen’s feast. At the banquet, the king asked again, “What is your petition, Esther? It will be granted to you, even to half the kingdom.”

“My petition is that if I have pleased the king, I invite you and Haman to come to another banquet I have prepared for tomorrow.”

Haman was delighted by all this attention from the queen. But as he walked home that evening, at the king’s gate he saw Mordecai, who still refused to bow to him. He was filled with anger again.

At his home, Haman called in his wife, Zeresh, and his friends and told them, “I have riches and children. The king has made me chief of all the princes and servants. Esther, the queen, has invited me personally to banquets she prepared for the king. But all this avails me nothing so long as I see Mordecai the Jew sitting at the king’s gate.”

His wife and friends said to him, “Order a gallows built, fifty cubits high.” This is around seventy-five feet. “And tomorrow ask the king for Mordecai to be hanged on it. Then you can merrily go to the banquet.”

So Haman ordered the gallows to be made.

That night, the king could not sleep. He commanded that the book of records be read to him. They read the section that recorded how Mordecai had warned of an evil plot to kill the king.

The king asked, “What honor was given to Mordecai for this service he did for me?”

The king’s servants said, “There was nothing done for him.”

King Ahasuerus asked, “Who is in the court right now?”

Haman was at the outer court, waiting to speak to the king about hanging Mordecai.

The king called him in and asked Haman, “What should be done for a man whom the king wishes to honor?”

Haman thought the king wanted to honor him, so he said, "Let royal apparel be brought that the king has worn, and the royal crown, and the king's horse. Give these to one of the king's most noble princes, to array the man whom the king wants to honor. Let the prince take the man through the streets of the city, proclaiming how the king is honoring him."

The king said to Haman, "Make haste, take the apparel and the horse as you have said and give this honor to Mordecai the Jew that sits at the king's gate. Do all that you have said for him."

Haman did as the king asked. He arrayed Mordecai in the king's clothes, put him on the king's horse, and took him through the streets of the city, proclaiming, "See how the king honors the man he wishes to reward!"

Afterward, Mordecai returned to the gate, and Haman hurried home, covering his head. He was upset. He told his wife and friends what had happened, and they all said, "You won't be able to prevail against Mordecai now."

While they were talking, the king's chamberlain came to escort Haman to the queen's feast.

At the banquet, the king again asked, "What is your petition, Queen Esther?"

"If I have found favor in your sight, please give me my life and the lives of my people. We are sold, I and my people, to be destroyed and to be killed."

"Who is it? Where is he that presumes to do this?" the king cried.

"My enemy is this wicked Haman sitting here."

The king was angry and stormed into the palace garden. Haman saw the king's anger and was afraid. He stood and rushed to the queen. He fell against her couch, begging for his life.

The king came back in and saw Haman. "Will he attack the queen in front of me?" he cried.

The king's servants grabbed Haman and covered his face.

The king's chamberlain said, "There are gallows at Haman's house, fifty cubits high, where Haman intended to hang Mordecai."

The king ordered that Haman be hanged there. They hanged Haman on the gallows intended for Mordecai.

The king's previous decree could not be revoked. But the king gave his ring to Mordecai, and with Esther, they composed a decree that was sent through all the land. The Jews were to be armed and able to defend themselves.

On the day Haman decreed all the Jews to be destroyed, the Jews were able to save themselves and triumph. The evil men who fought against them were destroyed.

Because Queen Esther was brave, she and Mordecai were able to save the Jews. To this day, the Jewish people celebrate the holiday Purim because they were saved on the day they would have been destroyed.

Read Queen Esther's story in

Esther 1–9

Chapter 10

Abish & the Queen

Be willing to act, like Abish

LONG, LONG ago, in the Lamanite land of Ishmael, Abish lived with her family. Her father had a vision that was sent from God. He shared this vision with Abish, and they were both converted to the Lord. But they were Lamanites, and none of the other Lamanites believed in God. The Lamanites were also a violent people, so Abish kept quiet about her conversion for her own safety.

Many years later, Abish worked as a servant for King Lamoni. She served his wife, the queen.

The king owned flocks of sheep and had other servants who took care of them. One day, robbers attacked while the king's sheep were drinking at the waters of Sebus. The sheep were scattered, and many were stolen. When the king heard, he was angry and had the servants in charge of the sheep killed as punishment for losing some of his flock.

Soon after, a Nephite came into the land. Nephites were enemies of the Lamanites, so he was captured and taken to the king. The Nephite's name was Ammon. King Lamoni asked Ammon if he wanted to live with the Lamanites.

"Yes," Ammon said. "I want to live with this people for a while. Maybe for the rest of my life."

This pleased the king so much, he had Ammon untied and even offered to give Ammon one of his daughters to marry.

"No," Ammon said, "But I will be your servant."

The king sent Ammon to watch his sheep.

On the third day after the Nephite's arrival, servants carried the king's lifeless body to the queen. He had dropped to the ground and lay like he were dead. The queen and the princesses and princes, their children, cried and mourned for their father. Most thought he was dead.

The servants who brought in the king told them what happened. Ammon had watched the king's sheep with the other servants. The robbers had attacked again, but this time, Ammon had defended them with his sling and sword. He cut off the arms of the attackers and killed several of them.

This amazed the king. He felt that no man could do something like this. He thought Ammon must be the Great Spirit and that Ammon had come to keep the king from killing his servants again.

When Ammon had come to the king, the king asked him where he had gotten this great power. Ammon taught King Lamoni about God. He told him about the plan of happiness.

After he had explained these things to the king, King Lamoni had cried out, "Oh, Lord, have mercy! The mercy you have shown to the Nephites, have on me and my people!"

Then he had fallen to the ground. There he lay, not moving. The queen and her children wept over him.

Abish was amazed when she heard the story. This Nephite was teaching of God. He had taught the king.

After two days, some wanted to bury the king, but the queen was not ready to give up on her husband. She asked the Nephite, Ammon, to come to her.

When he came in, he asked, "What do you want me to do?"

"The servants of my husband tell me that you are a prophet of a Holy God," the queen said. "And that you have the power to do many great works in His name. If this is the case, I want you to go in to see my husband. He has lain on his bed for two days and two nights. Some say he is not dead, but others say that he is and that he stinks. They say he should be placed in a sepulchre. But he doesn't stink to me."

Ammon, the Nephite, went in and looked at the king. He told the queen, "He is not dead. He sleeps in God. He will wake up tomorrow, so do not bury him." The Nephite then asked, "Do you believe me?"

"I have no other witnesses but you and the word of our servants, but I believe."

"Bless you," Ammon said, "for your great faith. There hasn't been faith as great as yours among all the Nephites."

The queen watched over the bed of the king all night. Abish watched with her. In the morning, the king did wake up. He stood and reached for his wife.

"Blessed be the name of God! And blessed are you," the king said to his wife. "For as sure as you are alive, I have seen my Redeemer, and He will come forth and be born of a woman. He shall redeem all mankind who believe in His name."

The king was filled with so much joy that he sunk down again and became unconscious. The queen collapsed as well, overpowered by the Spirit. Ammon fell to his knees and gave thanks to God for blessing the Lamanites with His Spirit. Ammon was overpowered too and sank to the ground.

The servants who had been watching the sheep with Ammon were there, and witnessing this, they were afraid and began to call out to God with their might. Each one was overcome by the Spirit of the Lord and fainted as well.

Abish stood among them as the people around her fainted. She knew it was the power of God, like her father had told her so many years before. She felt the Spirit and thought to herself, "This is my opportunity. If all the people see this miracle, they will believe in God."

So she ran out of the king's house and into the streets. She ran from house to house, calling out, "The power of God has overcome the king and queen! Come and see!"

The people she talked to went to the house of the king to see what she was talking about. Abish ran and told many people. She was filled with joy that so many of her people would be converted to the Lord.

She came back to the king's house. A large crowd had gathered there. But to her horror, Abish realized they were not being converted to the Lord. They were fighting. They were afraid and were yelling back and forth. They saw the king, the queen, the Nephite, and the servants all struck down. They looked dead.

Some thought this evil had happened because the king had let a Nephite stay in their land. Some said it was a punishment to the king for killing his servants because they had lost the sheep. The robbers who had attacked the sheep were also there, and they were angry with Ammon. One charged into the room, intending to kill Ammon with his sword. He fell down dead.

The crowd yelled back and forth, "Who has this great power? What does this mean?"

"He's the Great Spirit!"

"He's a monster!"

"He was sent by the Great Spirit to afflict us because of our sins. The Great Spirit always favors the Nephites. He's always delivering them from our armies and destroying us."

Abish's heart hurt, and her eyes filled with tears. The people were angry and yelling. She went to the queen and hoped she could wake her. Abish touched the queen's hands, and the queen did wake up.

She stood on her feet and cried out loudly, "Oh, blessed Jesus, who has saved me from an awful hell! Oh, blessed God, have mercy on this people!" She clasped her hands together and was filled with joy. The queen said more words that the people didn't understand. She reached down and took the king's hand. He woke and stood up.

King Lamoni saw that his people had gathered and were confused and angry. He went to them and began to teach them of God and Christ. Ammon and all the servants arose. They witnessed to the people what had happened to them.

"Our hearts are changed. We have no more desire to do evil."

Many had seen angels and talked with them. They told the people about God and His goodness.

Many of the people did not want to hear these things. They left. But many others stayed and listened to the king and queen, Ammon, Abish, and the other servants. Those who listened believed and were converted to the Lord. They were baptized, and God's Church was established in the land of the Lamanites for the first time. The Lord poured out His Spirit over all the Lamanites.

Because Abish saw an opportunity and acted quickly, many people were converted to the Lord. God had put His faithful Abish in the house of the king, and her actions helped establish God's Church in the land of the Lamanites.

All who were converted became a righteous and devoted people. Abish was no longer alone in her devotion to God.

Read Abish & the Queen's story in

Alma 17–19

Chapter 11

Elisabeth

Trust in God, like Elisabeth

LONG, LONG ago, in a city of Judea, Elisabeth lived with her husband, Zacharias. They were a righteous couple from the priestly line of Aaron and were well respected. They wanted and prayed for children, but they had grown old without having any.

Zacharias was serving at the temple in Jerusalem, and his name was drawn as the priest to burn incense in the inner temple that day. While he was there alone, burning the incense, the angel Gabriel came to him.

Gabriel said, "Thy prayer is heard. Your wife shall bear a son. You shall call his name John. Have joy and gladness! He shall be great in the sight of the Lord and filled with the Holy Ghost from his mother's womb. He will prepare the way for the Lord."

Zacharias said, "How can this happen? I'm old, and so is my wife."

The angel answered, "Because you do not believe my words, you shall be unable to speak until the day these things shall be performed."

The people outside of the temple wondered why Zacharias was taking so long. When he came out, he couldn't speak. The crowd was amazed.

After the days he was to serve at the temple were over, he left Jerusalem and traveled home to his wife. Elisabeth did become pregnant.

She stayed quietly in her home for five months. She was amazed and happy that she was finally going to have a baby.

In her sixth month, her young cousin Mary came to visit her. As soon as Elisabeth heard Mary's greeting, the baby in Elisabeth's

womb jumped and kicked. The baby was really excited. Elisabeth was filled with the Holy Ghost. The Spirit had let Elisabeth know that Mary was going to be the mother of the Savior.

She called out, "Blessed are you among women, and blessed is the fruit of your womb! How is this, that the mother of my Lord is coming to visit me? My baby is leaping for joy."

They were amazed and happy that they were both going to have miracle babies. Mary was a virgin and not yet married. The son she was carrying was from God. Elisabeth was blessed to know that Mary was the mother of the Messiah and that her own son had a great calling from God to prepare the people for the Messiah's coming.

Mary said a song of praise: "My soul magnifies the Lord. I rejoice in my God and Savior. He has regarded the low state of His handmaiden. All generations after me shall call me blessed."

Mary stayed three months with Elisabeth, until the end of Elisabeth's pregnancy, and then went home. When Elisabeth had her baby, her neighbors and relatives all rejoiced and were so happy for her.

When the baby was eight days old, they all came to give him a name. They wanted to name him Zacharias, after his father.

Elisabeth stopped them and said, "No, his name is John." Elisabeth knew the angel's instructions for her miracle son. She stood up to her friends and neighbors so that God's commands would be followed.

"But no one else in your family is named John. Why would you name him that?" they asked her.

They went to Zacharias. He asked for a writing tablet. He wrote down, "His name is John."

As soon as Zacharias wrote that, he was able to speak again.

He was so happy. He praised the Lord and prophesied that his son would do great things. "Child, you will be called the prophet of the highest, for you will go before the face of the Lord to prepare His ways. You'll give knowledge of salvation unto His people by the remission of their sins."

Sometime on that day, an angel came and ordained Elisabeth's son, John, with power to overthrow the kingdom of the Jews and to make straight the way of the Lord.

Elisabeth's trust in God enabled her to be the mother of one of the Lord's great prophets and be able to support and care for Mary in her early pregnancy with Christ. Her son, John, prepared the way for Jesus, and Jesus came to him to be baptized.

Read Elisabeth's story in
Luke 1 D&C 84:27–28

Chapter 12

Mary

Ponder over spiritual things, like Mary

LONG, LONG ago, in the city of Nazareth of Judea, there lived a beautiful young woman named Mary. She was engaged to be married to Joseph, a carpenter. They were both from the royal line of King David, but the Romans ruled Israel at this time. Mary was a princess by lineage, but she and Joseph lived normal lives in Nazareth.

One day, the angel Gabriel came to Mary and said to her, "Hail, Mary! The Lord is with you, and you are blessed among women."

Mary was amazed and troubled.

The angel continued, "Fear not. You have found favor with God, and you shall bear a son and name him Jesus. He shall be

great and will be called the Son of the Highest. God will give Him the throne of David, and His kingdom will have no end."

Mary asked, "How can this happen? I'm not married yet."

Gabriel answered, "The Holy Ghost will come over you, and God's power will overshadow you. Your baby will be the Son of God."

The angel also let Mary know that her older cousin Elisabeth, who didn't have any children, was finally pregnant and in her sixth month. He said, "For with God, nothing is impossible."

Mary was amazed by all this, but she said, "I am the handmaid of the Lord." She accepted the angel's word and calling.

After she became pregnant, she left Nazareth quickly and spent her first three months of pregnancy with her cousin Elisabeth. After she came back home, Joseph, her fiancé, discovered she was pregnant. He knew he was not the father. Joseph was a good man, and he didn't want to shame her in front of the whole town or to endanger her, so he decided to break off their engagement privately.

But an angel came to him in a dream. "Joseph, son of David," the angel said to him, "fear not to wed Mary. The baby she carries was conceived from the Holy Ghost. Call his name Jesus, for He will save His people from their sins."

When Joseph awoke, he did as the angel said, and Joseph and Mary were married.

Caesar Augustus was the Roman Emperor who ruled over most of the Middle East and Europe at this time. He decreed that all the people in his empire must be counted and taxed. All the people had to go to their hometowns to be registered. Joseph's family was from the small town of Bethlehem. He and Mary traveled to Bethlehem from Nazareth, a distance of about a hundred miles. Mary was at the end of her pregnancy, so she was large and uncomfortable on the journey. She went into labor, but when they reached the town, so many people had come in for the taxing that there was no room left for them in any of the inns in Bethlehem.

They stayed in a stable with the animals, where Mary gave birth to her son. She wrapped her newborn baby in swaddling

clothes and laid him to sleep in a manger, a box that animals would normally eat or drink from. They named the baby Jesus.

Later in the night, shepherds came and visited them. Angels had come and told them that the Savior had been born. The angels had sung praises to God. The shepherds followed the angel's directions and came to see the miraculous baby.

Mary pondered all these things in her heart.

Mary and Joseph were Jews and followed the law of Moses. Under the law of Moses, if a son was born first in a family, that son was dedicated to the Lord. So after a month of purification for Mary, they traveled to Jerusalem to present Jesus at the temple and offer a sacrifice of two turtledoves.

In the temple, an old man came up to them. He took the baby into his arms, blessed God, and said, "I can now die in peace. For the Lord told me that before I would die, I would see our salvation. This baby will be a light to the Gentiles and a glory to the people of Israel."

Joseph and Mary were amazed. The Holy Ghost had told the old man who their baby was. The man's name was Simeon. He told Mary, "This child is appointed for the fall and rise of many in Israel and for a sign. A sword will pierce through your soul. The thoughts of many shall be revealed."

Anna, a prophetess who served in the temple, witnessed this and came and rejoiced as well. She held up the baby to the crowd in the temple. "Those who look for redemption in Israel, look here!"

When Jesus was a toddler, Joseph and Mary were living in Bethlehem. A group of wise men from foreign lands came and visited them. They had seen a new star and had followed it until they found Jesus and Mary. They worshipped the young boy and gave him treasures—gifts of frankincense, gold, and myrrh.

Judea was ruled by Herod the king. He had been appointed by the Roman Emperor. In their travels, the Wise Men had first gone to King Herod and asked if he knew where the Messiah was to be born. The king's scholars had looked it up and said, "In Bethlehem." Herod the king had asked the Wise Men to come

back and tell him where the child was once they found him. He had said he wanted to worship the child as well.

But the Wise Men were warned in a dream not to tell Herod. They left and returned to their own country another way.

Herod was angry that the Wise Men never returned to him. He felt that this "promised Messiah" was a threat to his rule. He did not want a Messiah to come. To get rid of this threat, Herod had all the babies two years and younger in Bethlehem and the surrounding areas killed.

A dream came to Joseph as well. An angel told them to flee into Egypt, because Herod wanted to kill the baby. They left by night before Herod's soldiers came. They went into Egypt, and lived there until King Herod died.

After Herod died, an angel came to Joseph in a dream again and let him know it was safe to take Mary and young Jesus back to Judea. They settled in Galilee and raised Jesus there.

Every year, Mary and Joseph would travel to Jerusalem to celebrate the Feast of the Passover. The year Jesus was twelve, as they were coming back from Jerusalem, Mary and Joseph thought Jesus was traveling with friends in their group. But at the end of a day's travel, they discovered He was nowhere to be found. They went back to Jerusalem with anxious hearts and looked all over for Him for three days.

They finally found Him at the temple. He was with the teachers and learned men of the temple, listening to them and asking them questions. Everyone who listened to Jesus was amazed that a twelve-year-old boy could be as wise as Jesus was.

But Mary and Joseph were upset. "Son, why have you treated us this way? We've been worried and looking for you everywhere."

"Why have you been looking for me?" Jesus asked. "Didn't you know that I would be doing my Father's work?"

They didn't understand this, but Jesus came home with them and obeyed them. He grew tall and wise and in favor with God and man.

And Mary, as always, kept these things in her heart and thought about them deeply. She was blessed to be the mother of the Savior, and as she observed miracle after miracle happen around her, she stored them all up in her heart. She deepened her connection to God as she pondered the things of the Spirit.

Read Mary's story in

Luke 1–2
Matthew 1–2

Prophecy about Mary

Isaiah 7:14
1 Nephi 11:13–21
Mosiah 3:8
Alma 7:10

More on her life

John 2:2–5
Matthew 12:46; 13:54–55
Mark 3:31–32; 6:3
Luke 8:19
John 19:25–26
Acts 1:14

Chapter 13

Mary & Martha

Serve, like Martha
Thirst after things of the Spirit, like Mary

LONG, LONG ago, Martha and Mary lived together with their brother, Lazarus, in Bethany—a village two miles east of Jerusalem. The siblings were followers of Jesus. They loved Him, and He loved them.

One day, when Jesus was visiting their village, they invited Him and His followers to stay at their house. Martha bustled about being the hostess, making sure all of her guests were comfortable and getting their meals ready. She felt stressed with so many things to do. Why wasn't Mary helping her?

Martha found Mary sitting at Jesus's feet, listening to Him while He taught. Martha came over to them. "Lord, don't you

care that Mary has left me to serve alone? Tell her that she should help me."

"Martha, Martha," Jesus said, "You are worried about many things. But one thing is needed, and Mary has chosen that good thing, which cannot be taken from her." Jesus supported Mary in her choice to sit and learn of the things of God.

Later, near the end of Jesus's ministry, Lazarus became sick.

Jesus was several days' journey away from them. He was staying away from Bethany because the Jews in Jerusalem had wanted to stone Him. It would be dangerous for Jesus to go as near to Jerusalem as Bethany.

But Lazarus was so sick, his sisters feared he would die. They knew Jesus could heal him. Lazarus became so close to death that they risked sending for Jesus.

They sent a message that said, "Lord, Lazarus, whom you love and care for, is sick."

Days passed, and Jesus did not come.

Lazarus died.

Mary and Martha wept in grief. They buried Lazarus in a tomb, and their friends and neighbors mourned with them and visited them in their house.

Four days passed, and finally Jesus came. Martha heard Jesus was coming and went to meet Him outside the village. Mary stayed in the house.

"Lord, if you had been here, my brother would not have died," Martha said to Jesus. "But I know that even now, whatever you ask of God, He will give it to you."

Jesus said to Martha, "Your brother will rise again."

"I know he will rise again at the resurrection, at the last day."

Jesus answered, "I am the resurrection and the life. He who believes in me, though he was dead, yet shall he live. And whoever lives and believes in me shall never die. Do you believe this?"

"Yes, Lord," she said to Him. "I believe that you are the Christ, the Son of God, that should come into the world."

Martha left Jesus and went to Mary. She secretly told her, "The Master has come, and He calls for you."

Mary got up immediately and went out to Him. The friends and neighbors who were in the house saw Mary leaving quickly and thought she was going to go weep at the graveside. They followed her out, weeping.

Jesus was waiting outside the town in the same place Martha had met Him. When Mary reached Jesus, she fell down at His feet, crying.

"Lord, if you had been here, my brother would not have died."

Jesus groaned seeing Mary's misery. "Where have you laid him?" He asked.

The people said, "Lord, come and see."

Jesus wept.

"Look how He loved Lazarus!" the friends and neighbors said. "Couldn't this man, who has cured blindness, have prevented Lazarus from dying?"

Mary, Martha, and their neighbors led Jesus to the tomb, which was a cave with a stone covering it.

Jesus said, "Move the stone away."

But Martha said, "Lord, by this time, he stinks. He has been dead four days."

"Didn't I tell you, if you would believe, you would see the glory of God?" Jesus said. The people moved the stone away.

Jesus looked up and prayed, "Father, I thank Thee that thou hast heard me. I know Thou hearest me always. I say this for the people who stand nearby, that they may believe that Thou hast sent me."

And Jesus commanded in a loud voice, "Lazarus, come forth!"

Lazarus did. He was wrapped in grave clothes that bound his hands and feet, and his face was covered.

"Loose him," Jesus said, "and let him go."

Mary and Martha looked on in amazement. Their brother Lazarus was alive again! The crowd around them was astonished.

Many began to believe in Jesus. But some went and told the Jewish leaders what had happened. The leaders started planning how to put Jesus to death. They sent out orders that any person who knew where Jesus was should tell them so they could arrest Him. The chief priests wanted to put Lazarus and Jesus to death because so many people were believing in Jesus and weren't following the priests anymore.

Jesus left and no longer walked openly in Judea.

Six days before the Passover, Jesus returned to Bethany. He visited the house of Simon the leper. Martha, Mary, and Lazarus came to dinner with Jesus, His disciples, and Simon.

Martha served the supper, and Lazarus sat at the table with Jesus.

Mary had a pound of spikenard—expensive perfume oil—in an alabaster jar. She had been saving it.

During the dinner, and in front of all of the guests, Mary broke open her jar and poured the spikenard oil over Jesus's head and feet. She rubbed the oil into His feet with her hair. The whole house was filled with the smell of the perfume oil.

Where they lived at this time, people used oil in their hair to groom it. They also wore sandals and walked on dry and dusty roads. Washing the feet of guests and rubbing oil into their feet like a lotion was a courtesy and a way to honor a guest. When Mary used this expensive and wonderful-smelling oil to anoint Jesus's head and feet and then wiped His feet with her hair, she was giving Him the highest honor she could. She showed her love and admiration for Him to all.

Judas Iscariot was one of the Apostles of Jesus. He was their treasurer and kept all the money Jesus and His disciples had. He also liked to steal from their money.

Judas objected to what Mary was doing. "What a waste," he said. "This oil could have been sold for three hundred pence and the money given to the poor."

"Leave her alone," Jesus told him. "Why are you troubling her? She has done a good work for me. The poor are always with you. You may serve them at any time. But I will not always be with you. By pouring this ointment on me, she has prepared me for my burial."

Spikenard was an oil often used to prepare the dead for burial, along with myrrh.

"Wherever my gospel shall be preached," Jesus said, "in the whole world, and in the generations to come, Mary shall be remembered for what she has done for me today."

Judas was offended by Jesus's words. That night after the meal, he went secretly to the Jewish leaders and offered to betray and deliver Jesus to them. The chief priests were glad Judas would do this for them. In exchange, they agreed to pay him thirty pieces of silver.

In the hard days to come, Jesus would be crucified and resurrected. Mary and Martha would get through those days because of the strength of their testimonies of Jesus and the support of their brother Lazarus, whom Jesus had returned to them.

Read Mary & Martha's story in

Matthew 26:6–16
Mark 14:3–11
Luke 10:38–42
John 11:1–46; 12:2–11

Chapter 14

Mary Magdalene

Stand as a witness of Christ, like Mary Magdalene

LONG, LONG ago, there was a young woman named Mary from Magdala, which was by the Sea of Galilee. She was called Mary Magdalene. Mary was sick in both mind and body. Jesus healed her.

Mary was so happy to be healed. She followed after Jesus. She joined a group of women from Galilee who traveled with Jesus and the disciples, taking care of them and paying for food and clothing for them out of their own money. Mary loved Jesus very much.

The Jewish leaders hated Jesus. They feared people would follow Him and they would lose their power and influence. They ordered His arrest. It was dangerous for Jesus to be near

Jerusalem. Nevertheless, Jesus came to Jerusalem to celebrate the Passover. When He arrived riding a young donkey, the people in the streets celebrated, laying their clothes in the street to cushion His way, waving palm fronds, and singing songs.

Jesus was in the city for several days. He taught daily at the temple. But the morning after the Passover Feast, Mary awoke early and heard horrible news. Jesus had been arrested! Judas Iscariot, one of His trusted Apostles, had betrayed Him and led the Jewish leaders to Him by night. They were taking Him before Pilate that morning, seeking to put Him to death. Mary's stomach clenched, and her chest felt tight with fear.

But there was some hope left. Pilate could let Jesus go. Pontius Pilate was the Roman governor of Judea. Rome ruled Israel, and under Roman law, only Pilate had the legal right to order someone killed.

An angry crowd gathered outside Pilate's palace, riled up by the Jewish priests and leaders. After speaking with Jesus and hearing His accusers, Pilate didn't think Jesus deserved death. He was willing to have Him whipped and set free.

Pilate had Jesus whipped. The Roman soldiers who did it mocked Jesus, putting a purple robe and a crown made of thorns on Him and calling Him the "King of the Jews."

Pilate showed Jesus to the crowd, giving them the option to let Jesus live. "I find no fault in Him," Pilate said.

The mob yelled out, "Crucify Him! Crucify Him!" They wanted Jesus to be crucified, a Roman method of torture and execution that was designed to be slow, painful, and public.

"Crucify Him! Crucify Him!" the crowd continued to yell. They would not stop yelling it.

Pilate washed his hands with water in front of the crowd, saying, "I am innocent of the blood of this just person." He ordered Jesus to be put to death, as the Jews wanted.

Mary tried to stay back in the crowd. It was a dangerous, angry crowd that jostled and pushed. But she wanted to keep Jesus in sight. The Roman soldiers put the top piece of Jesus's cross on His back for Him to carry to where He would be killed.

But He dropped it as the crowd pushed and spit on Him. So the soldiers grabbed a man from the crowd and made him carry the cross piece as they left the city to go to Golgotha, "the place of the skull."

Golgotha was a hill near where people were buried. It was on the road to Jerusalem. There, they nailed Jesus to the cross with His arms outstretched. It was about nine in the morning when Jesus was crucified. Two other men were crucified with Him. They were thieves.

Mary Magdalene stood and watched. With her were Mary— Jesus's mother—and several other women who followed Jesus. John, Jesus's Apostle, stood with Jesus's mother. The other Apostles were in hiding. They didn't want to be killed too.

But the women stood by and witnessed. They didn't leave Jesus alone.

Jesus saw His mother, the women, and John. He said to His mother, Mary, "He is now your son." To John, He said, "She is now your mother." Jesus wanted John to take care of His mother from then on.

People passed by Jesus and mocked Him. "If you are the Son of God, come down from the cross!"

Mary Magdalene knew Jesus was the Son of God. But He didn't come down off the cross.

"He saved others, but He can't save Himself!" the mocking people said.

"If He comes down from that cross, then we'll believe He is the Messiah!"

Hours passed. Agonizing, long, hot hours under the sun. But at noon, darkness suddenly came over the sky. The sun was covered.

Three more hours passed—the longest hours Mary would ever live.

Jesus cried out, “My God, my God, why hast Thou forsaken me?”

Mary could tell Jesus was in pain. And she couldn’t help him.

Suddenly, Jesus yelled out with a loud voice, “Father, it is finished! Thy will is done. Into Thy hands I commend my spirit.” Jesus bowed His head, and He died.

The earth was suddenly shaking underneath them. An earthquake! The women grabbed each other, trying to stay upright.

The centurion, the leader of the Roman soldiers, looked with amazement. “Truly this was the Son of God.”

The sky cleared. The sun came out again. But Jesus was dead.

Jewish law didn’t allow dead bodies to hang in the open overnight. Also, their Sabbath began when the sun went down. They had to get Jesus’s body down from the cross and buried before the sun set.

Joseph of Arimathea, a rich man who had kept his conversion to Jesus a secret until then, went to Pilate and asked for permission to bury Jesus’s body. Pilate was amazed that Jesus would be dead already. It usually took much longer than six hours to die by crucifixion. To be sure Jesus was dead, the soldiers pierced Him through the side with a spear.

Pilate gave permission to Joseph of Arimathea to take Jesus’s body. A man named Nicodemus helped Joseph take Jesus’s body down from the cross. They took Him to Joseph’s own tomb nearby. It was new and in a beautiful garden. Mary and some of the other women followed. They wrapped Jesus in clean linen, with myrrh and aloe. But they did it quickly because the sun was going down. The men pushed a large stone in front of the door to the tomb.

Mary Magdalene and another Mary, the mother of some of Jesus’s disciples, sat in front of the tomb. Mary Magdalene felt numb and drained. It was the Sabbath now, and they wouldn’t be able to finish tending to Jesus’s body until the first day of the week dawned.

Jesus was dead.

Mary spent the Sabbath quietly. The women prepared spices and ointments, getting them ready for the next day, when they could go back to the tomb to take care of Jesus's body again.

Mary didn't sleep well Saturday night. She got up before the dawn on Sunday and gathered her things to go to the tomb. The other women went with her.

As they walked, they worried, "Who will roll the stone away from the door for us?" The stone was heavy. When they got there, however, the stone had already been moved.

The tomb was empty. Jesus's body was gone!

The women ran to tell Jesus's disciples. Mary ran to Peter and John, two of Jesus's head Apostles.

"They have taken away the Lord out of the sepulchre, and we don't know where they have laid Him!" she panted.

Peter and John ran to the tomb. Mary followed them. Tears blinded her eyes, and sobs choked her throat. John reached the tomb door first and stooped down to look in. When Peter reached the door, they both went in. They saw the linen that had wrapped Jesus was still lying there, the cloth that had been around His face lying at the head. They didn't know what to do. His body was gone. Peter and John walked home again.

But Mary stayed standing outside the tomb, tears streaming down her face.

She stooped down to look into the tomb again and saw two angels in white, sitting where Jesus's body had lain, one at the head and one at the foot.

They asked her, “Lady, why are you crying?”

“Because they have taken away my Lord, and I don’t know where they have laid Him,” she said.

Mary turned and looked behind her, and she saw a man standing outside the tomb.

“Lady, why are you crying? Who are you looking for?” the man asked.

Her eyes were filled with tears. She thought the man must be the gardener. “Sir, if you have moved Him, tell me where you have laid Him and I will take Him away.”

“Mary.”

Mary turned herself completely. She knew that voice. She looked at Him with clear eyes.

It was Jesus.

“Master!” she cried. It was Him. He was alive. She reached for Him.

“Don’t hold me, Mary,” Jesus said. “I have not yet ascended to my Father. But go to my brethren and tell them that I ascend to my Father, and your Father, and to my God, and your God.”

Mary did. Her heart was full of joy as she walked back. Jesus was resurrected!

She told the disciples she had seen Jesus and He was alive. She told them what He had said to her. They didn’t believe her.

But the other women of their group who went to the tomb also spoke to the angels. Jesus appeared to them as well.

Throughout the day, reports came back. Jesus had talked and traveled with two of His disciples as they walked to a town, Emmaus, seven miles away. He had eaten with them.

Jesus’s Apostles didn’t know what to think.

But Mary knew. Her eyes were no longer blurred with tears. Her Lord was alive, and He had spoken to her.

She had been the first person to speak to the resurrected Christ. He had seen her crying and had come to comfort her.

That evening, Jesus appeared to His Apostles, and over the next forty days, He continued to appear and prepare them to go and take His gospel to the world.

But Mary Magdalene had been first. She stood as witness to the greatest miracle.

Mary stood and saw Jesus of Nazareth die, saw Him buried, and saw His empty tomb. He had come to her and spoken to her. He was alive again. Her witness stands strong, recorded in the scriptures.

Read Mary Magdalene's story in

Matthew 27–28
Mark 15–16
Luke 8:2
Luke 23–24
John 19–20

Chapter 15

Lucy Mack Smith

Seek after the truth of God, like Lucy Mack Smith

NOT SO long ago, Lucy Mack was born in New Hampshire, four days after the Declaration of Independence was signed and the war started that would establish the United States of America. Her father and teen brothers served in the Revolutionary War. She grew up with an adventurous and hardworking father and a mother who educated her and taught her about God, love, and prayer.

When Lucy was a young woman, her sisters died of illnesses. She turned to God for comfort. She wanted to be baptized and join a church. But a thought stopped her.

"If I remain out of any church," she thought, "all religious people will say that I am of the world. If I join any one church, the rest will all declare that I am in the wrong. . . . How shall I decide? The Church of Christ was not like any of them."

Eventually, she decided to be baptized by a preacher but not actually join a church, as none of them seemed quite right.

She married Joseph Smith Sr. in 1796, and they had eleven children. Two died as babies, and nine grew up to adulthood.

After she had her first two little boys, Alvin and Hyrum, she got sick. She was close to dying. She later wrote, "I begged and pleaded with the Lord that He would spare my life so I might bring up my children and comfort the heart of my husband. During the night, I made a solemn covenant with God."

Lucy promised the Lord she would find a religion that would help her serve Him, wherever it was to be found, even if it was to be "obtained from heaven by prayer and faith."

A voice spoke to her. "Seek and ye shall find, knock and it shall be opened unto you. Let your heart be comforted. Ye believe in God, believe also in me.'"

Her mother, who was helping to take care of her, came in and looked at her. She cried out, "Lucy, you are better!"

Lucy answered, "Yes, Mother, the Lord will let me live."

Lucy and Joseph started out their married life with money and land, but a dishonest man stole from them and left them poor. They worked hard and paid their debts, but supporting their family was hard.

When Lucy's fifth child, Joseph Jr., was seven, illness swept through the family. Typhus fever raged in all the children. Her eldest daughter, Sophronia, almost died, but Lucy and her husband knelt and prayed for their daughter, and she lived.

The fever lodged in young Joseph's leg, however, and he was in constant pain for weeks. The doctors wanted to amputate his leg. His father insisted they try to cut out the bad parts of the bone instead. Joseph Jr. refused to be tied down or to drink alcohol to dull the pain. He sent his mother out of the room; he didn't want her to see him in pain. His father held him while the surgeons cut into his leg.

Joseph screamed as they cut into his bone, and Lucy burst back into the room. "Oh, Mother, go back! Go back!" young Joseph cried. "I do not want you to come in! I will tough it out if you will go." His mother had a hard time staying away, but the operation worked, and Joseph's leg recovered. He spent three years on crutches.

During those three years, their crops kept failing. They would plant, the weather would turn bad, and their plants wouldn't grow. And then 1815 was the year without a summer. A volcano erupted on the other side of the world and cloaked the sun so much in ash that there was freezing snow all over the world in July. No crops grew. The Smith family had to move to better land.

Lucy's husband went ahead of them to New York State to prepare their new farm. He hired a man, Mr. Howard, to drive their wagon and take Lucy and the Smith children the three hundred miles from their Vermont home to their new one in Palmyra. Lucy packed up the house and put the kids and all she could take in the wagon. They had little money left—just enough to get to Palmyra.

Soon after Lucy and her then eight children started on their journey, they discovered that their teamster, Mr. Howard, was a cruel and evil man. He made little Joseph, who was hobbling on crutches, walk behind the wagon for miles in the snow so that Mr. Howard could offer rides to two young women from another family they were traveling with. He hit Joseph's brothers when they objected. Lucy clutched her baby and didn't know what to do. They tried to be patient; they depended on this man to get them to New York.

Mr. Howard used their money to drink and gamble in taverns at night, and with one hundred miles still left on their journey, the money ran out. In the morning, Mr. Howard started to throw their belongings out of the wagon. He was going to steal the horses and wagon!

Lucy finally confronted him. "What are you doing?"

"The money is gone. I will go no farther."

Lucy called on the people nearby to witness. "The wagon and horses are mine! This man is trying to take them and leave me destitute with eight little children. I forbid you, Mr. Howard, from stirring one step with my wagon or horses. I shall take charge of the team myself! As for you, sir, I have no use for you."

Thankfully, there were enough people watching that Mr. Howard had to walk away.

By selling or trading their belongings, Lucy was able to get the family to Palmyra. But the last day of the journey, Joseph was in another sleigh with the family they were traveling with. It was the last vehicle in their company. The driver decided he didn't like Joseph and knocked him out of the sleigh. The driver drove on and left Joseph bleeding in the snow. Joseph's mother was in their wagon near the front and didn't know this happened. Joseph was alone and barely conscious.

A stranger picked him up and carried him the rest of the way to Palmyra.

Lucy was so happy and relieved to be reunited with her husband and all her children. They didn't have any money, but they had each other. They were able to settle in Palmyra and build their lives again.

The people of New England were having a religious revival. All were "getting religion." Lucy wanted to be close to God and to have a church her whole family could join and be united in. But Lucy still didn't know which church was right. She and her children tried them all.

The churches fought against each other, each vying for followers. The members of one church were often mean to the members of another. Lucy eventually settled on the Presbyterian faith and joined with three of her children.

Lucy worried about her husband. He was a good, spiritual man who was close to God, but he didn't like any of the churches and refused to go to them.

Her son Joseph was fourteen now and really wanted to find the right church to join. He went to the meetings and thought a lot about which church might be correct. He read in the Bible, looking for guidance.

One day, he was gone the whole morning. Lucy was in the house when he walked in looking pale and weak. He leaned against the fireplace.

"Joseph, what's the matter?" Lucy asked.

Joseph shook his head. "Never mind," he said, "all is well—I am well enough off." Then he told her, "I have learned for myself that Presbyterianism is not true."

Joseph had seen a vision.

Joseph confided to a preacher about having seen a vision, and the preacher dismissed it. The preacher told him, "There are no such things as visions or revelations in these days; all such things ceased with the Apostles! There will never be any more of them."

But Joseph had seen a vision, and he wouldn't deny it.

Rumors flooded the town about Joseph. The family felt the jeers and scorn of their neighbors. But Lucy and the family stood by Joseph.

A few years later, Joseph saw another vision. An angel named Moroni came to him as he lay in bed and told him of a record written on gold plates and hidden in a hill. He was to translate the record and publish it to the world. It contained truth the world was missing. It was the record of an ancient people of America, and it contained the gospel of Jesus Christ in a pure, unaltered form.

The angel told Joseph to tell his father about the vision, and two days later, they gathered the whole family together and told them the whole story.

Joseph wasn't ready to get the plates yet, but he would continue to receive instructions from time to time. Every evening, Lucy and her husband would gather their children together and listen with excitement as Joseph described what had been shown to him of the ancient inhabitants of America: their dress, the animals they rode, the structure of their cities and buildings, their mode of warfare, and their religious worship. He knew things about them as if he had lived with them.

A few months later, Lucy's oldest son, Alvin, died of a sudden illness and bad medicine. The family was devastated. Alvin had been Joseph's most enthusiastic supporter, and now that he was gone, just thinking about the gold plates made the whole family sad.

Several years passed. Joseph married Emma Hale. The following September, Joseph was finally ready to get the plates. He kept them safe and hidden, and Lucy and her family helped him keep them from being stolen by wicked men who wanted the gold.

Joseph translated the plates and published them as the Book of Mormon. He was called by God to be a prophet and restore Jesus Christ's true Church on the earth. Joseph formally organized the Church on April 6, 1830.

Lucy was so happy to finally have a true religion her family could be united with. She and the whole family were baptized. Her husband, Joseph Smith Sr., served as the first Patriarch of the Church.

Lucy supported the Church in any way she could. She became a mother to all the Saints who joined and came to gather with the Church. She looked on The Church of Jesus Christ of Latter-day Saints as her family's endeavor and did all she could to help it grow and succeed.

She was called Mother Smith by the Saints.

In 1836, Joseph was in the new temple at Kirtland, Ohio. He had a marvelous vision of the celestial kingdom. Adam and Abraham were there, and so were Joseph's brother Alvin and his father and mother. Lucy would live with God and Jesus in the celestial kingdom.

Lucy lived until she was eighty. She saw a lot of hardship, and many of her children died before her. After Joseph died, she wrote a history of his life, their family, and the founding of the Church. It is a vital record that gives us important insights into their lives.

Lucy's prayers to find the true religion of God were answered. She supported her son in his divine calling, and the true Church of God was restored, never to be taken from the earth again.

Read Lucy Mack Smith's story in

D&C 137:5

Joseph Smith—History

Lucy Mack Smith, *The History of Joseph Smith by His Mother*

The Joseph Smith Papers: History, 1838–1856, volume A-1 [23 December 1805–30 August 1834]; Lucy Mack Smith, History, 1845; Lucy Mack Smith, History, 1844–1845.

Chapter 16

Emma Hale Smith

Be an elect lady, like Emma

Not so long ago, Emma Hale was born in Harmony, Pennsylvania, as the seventh child of her family. She was gangly as a teenager, but as she reached her twenties, she grew into her height and became a beautiful, elegant woman. She loved to sing and had a clear soprano voice. She was educated and worked as a schoolteacher in her town.

Her father was a prosperous farmer with a large house he ran as an inn. That is how she first met Joseph Smith Jr. in 1825. He was in town to work for a local man and stayed at their house. Joseph and Emma liked each other, and Joseph returned several times to court her after the job in town was done. After knowing

each other for two years, they fell in love and wanted to get married.

Emma's father said no.

There were lots of rumors about Joseph Smith. He claimed to see visions and find gold records in hills. Emma's father didn't think he would be a good husband for her.

But Joseph had told Emma about his visions. He told her how he had been called of God. He had a great work to do for the Lord. Emma believed him. She wanted to marry him and help him with his work.

So Joseph and Emma eloped.

They went across state lines and married in the home of Squire Thomas Tarbill in South Bainbridge, New York State, on January 18, 1827.

They moved in with Joseph's family, where Emma began a lifelong friendship with Joseph's mother, Lucy.

On September 22, it was time for Joseph to receive the gold plates from the angel Moroni. Joseph and Emma borrowed a wagon and took it to the hill where the plates were buried. Emma waited in the wagon while Joseph went up the hill. When he came down again, he had the plates in a bag. They had to carefully hide them because many people wanted to steal them.

They were able to keep the plates safe, but it became too dangerous for Joseph in his hometown, so they left and went back to Emma's family. Her father had reconciled enough with his new son-in-law now to help them find a place to live and to help protect them, since Emma's hometown became hostile toward them too.

When they were settled into their new home in Harmony, Joseph began to work on translating the gold plates. Emma was his scribe, writing his words as he read out loud.

The angel Moroni had commanded Joseph not to show the plates to anybody without his permission. This included Emma. She never saw the plates.

But she did get to hold them under their cloth wrappings and feel their weight. She traced their outline with her finger and felt the plates shift under her touch. But she was strong and never lifted up the cloth to look at them, because God had said not to.

Emma became pregnant with her first child. She and Joseph were so excited to have a baby. But when she went into labor in June 1828, it was difficult. Little Alvin was born, but he only lived a few hours. Emma cried and mourned as they buried their baby.

Progress on translating the plates was slow. A man named Oliver Cowdery came to them in April the next year. He'd heard about the plates from Joseph's family, and he wanted to help. He became Joseph's scribe, and the translating went faster.

But Harmony was too dangerous for them now. Mobs of angry men didn't like them and threatened them. They moved to Fayette, New York, in May, and Joseph was finally able to finish the translation.

They published the translation as the Book of Mormon in March 1830.

In April, Joseph officially founded The Church of Jesus Christ of Latter-day Saints. They began to baptize people into the Church. Emma got baptized.

People in the places where they lived didn't like them. The people harassed and bullied them. Joseph and Emma had to move a lot to stay safe. The Lord protected them.

However, they didn't have much money or many chances to earn more. This worried Emma.

In July, the Lord said in a revelation to Joseph that he would not be blessed with talents in money and temporal things, "for this is not thy calling." In their lives, their business and monetary ventures failed often, and this caused a lot of heartache and strife. But as long as Joseph focused on his calling as a prophet, the Lord made sure they were okay.

The Lord sent a revelation specifically for Emma. It is recorded in Doctrine and Covenants section 25.

The Lord said to her, "Thou art an elect lady, whom I have called."

Jesus Christ told Emma to support and comfort her husband. He called her to teach in the Church and to compile a book of hymns. The Lord said His soul delighted in singing that comes from the heart. "The song of the righteous is a prayer unto me."

He encouraged her to be happy, to not be prideful, and to "let [her] soul delight in [her] husband."

If Emma kept the Lord's commandments, she would receive "a crown of righteousness."

Emma worked to keep God's commandments. She was dedicated to helping Joseph with his work as prophet.

In 1831, Emma gave birth to twins, Thaddeus and Louisa. But they came too early and didn't survive. They died the day they were born. Joseph and Emma were so heartbroken.

Another sister in the Church, Julia Murdock, also had twins. But she died. The twins' father couldn't take care of them well by himself, so he offered the babies to Joseph and Emma to adopt. They took them in, and they loved these babies. They named them Joseph and Julia.

A few months later, the babies had measles. Joseph and Emma had taken care of them all day and were now trying to get some sleep. Joseph had his adopted baby son in the bed with him.

A mob of angry men broke into their home and dragged Joseph out. The men's faces were painted black. The baby boy was left screaming and cold.

The evil men hurt Joseph. They spread pine tar over his skin and covered him in feathers. This was called tarring and feathering. It was a cruel way to humiliate someone.

When the mob finally left Joseph alone, he dragged himself home. Emma fainted at the sight of all his injuries. She and their friends had to work through the night to get the tar off of Joseph. They used lard to soften the tar and scraped it off his skin. Joseph was left burned, raw, and bruised, with a chipped tooth.

The next morning was Sunday. Joseph got dressed and taught in church despite it all.

Their baby boy had gotten so cold, however, that he got sicker and died a few days later.

Emma lost many babies. She and Joseph had eleven children together, including their adopted twins, but only five of those children reached adulthood. In 1832, Joseph Smith III was born in Kirtland, their fourth biological child and the first to grow up.

While Emma and Joseph were living in Kirtland, Joseph taught the brethren of the Church in the home where they were staying. Chewing and smoking tobacco was common at this time, even with the Saints. Emma was annoyed at having to clean up the tobacco stains after the men left. It was stinky and dirty.

Joseph was concerned too, so he prayed to the Lord about it. God answered with the Word of Wisdom. After this revelation, members of the Church gradually stopped using tobacco, alcohol, and coffee and tried to eat more healthily, as God counseled.

In 1834, Emma received a patriarchal blessing from her father-in-law, Joseph Smith Sr., who was Patriarch to the Church. One of the things her blessing promised was, "Thou shalt see many days, yea, the Lord will spare thee till thou art satisfied, for thou shalt see thy Redeemer."

Emma would have a long life and would see Jesus Christ before she died.

Emma put together the book of hymns God had asked for, and it was published in time to be used for the Kirtland Temple dedication in 1835.

Emma had two more sons who lived: Frederick, born in 1836, and Alexander, born in 1838.

Evil men often put Joseph in prison. He wrote letters to Emma from prison. In one, he said to her, "My heart is entwined around yours forever and ever." Joseph and Emma loved each other very much.

God had instructed Joseph to write a translation of the Bible so God could restore information that had been lost from it. In the winter of 1839, Joseph was in prison again when Emma was forced to flee from Far West with her children. Emma had the

Bible translation with her. To protect the papers, she wore them in sacks tied under her skirts. She held her two youngest sons in her arms, with seven-year-old Julia and six-year-old Joseph III walking beside her, hanging onto her skirts as they crossed the thinly frozen Mississippi River on foot to get to safety.

Emma and Joseph were reunited, and they worked together with the Saints to found Nauvoo, a new city on the swampy banks of the Mississippi River in Illinois. Here, they were finally able to stay and build a home. Emma took in the needy. She helped the sick and cared for them.

Emma had another son, Don Carlos, in 1840, but he died a year later.

Joseph organized the Female Relief Society of Nauvoo on March 17, 1842. He called Emma to be the first president of the Relief Society. She formally began teaching in the Church, fulfilling God's revelation from a decade earlier.

Emma told the sisters in that first meeting, "We are going to do something extraordinary." Emma set up the standards of compassionate service, charity, and women teaching and helping others that Relief Society sisters continue to strive for.

In 1843, God gave a special revelation. It was about celestial marriage. Under God's priesthood authority, men and women could be sealed together in marriage through all eternity. Several parts of the revelation were directed to Emma. Emma and Joseph were sealed together.

Emma was also the first woman to receive the temple endowment, and she helped teach the next women who received theirs.

Throughout their marriage, Joseph had often been arrested and put into prison by men who were trying to use the law to stop Joseph and the Church from progressing. Again and again, Joseph was torn from Emma's side by evil men who treated him badly and imprisoned him. The Lord would help Joseph, and he would escape or be released when the men couldn't twist the law enough to hold him anymore. Every time, Emma ached and worried until Joseph was back with her again.

But in 1844, the Lord allowed Joseph to be killed. Joseph was imprisoned in Carthage Jail with a few other leaders of the Church when a mob attacked with guns and shot him. His brother Hyrum was also killed.

Joseph was a prophet, and he sealed his testimony with his life.

Emma's husband was dead. She cried and mourned. She was left desolate.

Emma was pregnant. Her last son, David Hyrum, would be born five months after his father died.

Brigham Young became the next prophet. The Saints completed the Nauvoo Temple, and many were able to receive their endowments. But they were still being persecuted. Bad people bullied and threatened them. They were in danger. Brigham Young directed the Saints to cross the Mississippi River and head for the Rocky Mountains. The Church members left their beautiful city and their temple for safety in the sparsely populated mountains and deserts outside the United States.

But Emma was exhausted. She didn't want to move. She said, "I was too tired to go west." She had a home here, after having been uprooted again and again. Without Joseph to help her any more, she couldn't face moving one more time, to a place no one knew much about. She wanted to stay home and raise her children in peace.

Joseph's mother, Lucy, was too old and frail for the journey as well. She stayed with Emma, and Emma took care of her until she died.

Nauvoo emptied of people.

Emma stayed in their big house and lived quietly with her children and Mother Smith. Two years after Joseph's death, she married Major Lewis C. Bidamon, a nonmember who was a friend. He took care of her and the children. They ran a store and a hotel out of the Mansion House, where Emma lived. But without many people living in Nauvoo, they didn't earn much money from it.

Lucy Smith had admired Emma. She wrote a tribute to her. She said that Emma was the most courageous woman she had ever seen and that she met hardship with "unflinching courage, zeal, and patience."

Emma lived until she was seventy-four, a long life like her patriarchal blessing had promised.

But one promise had yet to be fulfilled.

A few days before she died, Emma told her nurse she'd had a dream. In the dream, Joseph had told her, "Emma, come with me."

Joseph took her to a beautiful mansion. Her baby Don Carlos was there, and she was able to hold him. "Joseph," Emma asked, "where are the rest of my children?"

"Emma, be patient and you shall have all of your children."

And then Emma met Jesus Christ.

Through that vision, the promises given to Emma in her patriarchal blessing were fulfilled.

Emma died and was reunited in the spirit world with Joseph and their children who had died before her.

Emma was an elect lady. She stood by Joseph Smith through trials, injustice, and suffering. Her support enabled him to translate the Book of Mormon and restore Jesus Christ's full gospel to the earth once more.

Read Emma Hale Smith's story in

D&C 25 D&C 89

"Section 89 The Word of Wisdom," *Doctrine and Covenants Student Manual* (Salt Lake City: The Church of Jesus Christ of Latter-day Saints, 2002), 206–11.

Valeen Tippetts Avery and Linda King Newell, "The Elect Lady: Emma Hale Smith," *Ensign*, September 1979.

Gracia N. Jones, "My Great-Great-Grandmother, Emma Hale Smith," *Ensign*, August 1992.

Carol Cornwall Madsen, "'My Dear and Beloved Companion': The Letters of Joseph and Emma Smith," *Ensign*, September 2008.

Patriarchal Blessing and Fulfillment

Patriarchal blessing given to Emma Hale Smith, 9 December 1834, Kirtland, Ohio. Joseph Smith Sr., Oliver Cowdery, clerk and recorder. *Patriarchal Blessing Book,* 1:4-5, Archives of The Church of Jesus Christ of Latter-day Saints.

The Reorganized Church of Jesus Christ of Latter Day Saints, "Emma Smith's Last Testimony," *Saints Herald* (Independence, Missouri, Beruary 1879), vol. 26, 289.

Alexander Hale Smith, sermon given 1 July 1903, Bottlineau, North Dakota; reprinted in *Zion's Ensign*, 31 December 1903.

Conclusion

LIKE THE faithful women who have gone before us, we are princesses of God striving for queens' crowns. God has said that we are His work and His glory (Moses 1:39). We can be "a crown of glory in the hand of the Lord" (Isaiah 62:3), and like Emma Smith, we can be given "a crown of righteousness" (D&C 25:15).

As we rely on our Savior, Jesus Christ, we become the jewels in Heavenly Father's crown.

"They shall be mine, saith the Lord of hosts, in that day when I make up my jewels" (Malachi 3:17; see also D&C 101:3).

Heavenly Father has great work for us to do while we live on this earth. We are to build Heavenly Father's kingdom here. We build His kingdom through every righteous choice we make.

Sometimes the actions in our lives will seem small, simple, normal, and maybe even boring. But that is how God does many mighty things.

Like our sisters of old, we will go through trials and hardships, difficult decisions and difficult situations. And like those daughters of God who chose good and were blessed, as we choose good, we will be blessed.

We are living in the last days. It is our privilege to build God's kingdom, Zion, on the earth and to prepare the world for Jesus Christ to come again.

By learning from the experiences of God's righteous daughters and by following the directions of the Holy Ghost, we will be able to accomplish everything God needs us to do and will receive those crowns of righteousness.

Acknowledgments

My thanks to Heavenly Father and Jesus Christ for everything. My thanks to the great women of the scriptures for their lives and to the recorders of the scriptures for writing it down for us. My thanks to the preservers and translators of the scriptures. We can have access to them now, after centuries.

Thank you to my wonderful husband, Karl, who felt the weight of my contract and impending deadlines worse than I did and supported me with many "You should be working on your book" prods. Thank you, Karl, for your patience when I have five hundred ideas for new projects and for helping me prioritize.

Thank you to my parents, who bemusedly helped me go for my dreams when I wanted to be a writer, and then an artist, and now a writing artist. Great thanks to my mother and my sister Marissa for proofreading every story.

Thanks to Cedar Fort for being a good company that works hard to produce wonderful things. Thanks to my editor Emily for being excited about the proposal and liking it when I finished. Thanks to Shawnda, Jessica, and Heidi for their hard work on this book and all the beautiful books they work on.

Thank you to all the wonderful people who posed as photo-reference models for me! Thanks to my Lewis cousins for posing after Easter dinner for multiple scenes, and my beautiful coworkers who willingly gathered and posed for Esther praying with her maidservants and several other complex character interactions. Many illustrations came together because of my wonderful models.

Many thanks to my Relief Society counselors, who willingly help and accept assignments as I try to balance everything. I was called as Relief Society president in my ward (!) in the middle of writing this book and only because of their great help was I able to get it all done. Great thanks again to the Lord, who provided small miracles so that this book was able to be finished. Thank you!

About the Author & Illustrator

Rebecca J. Greenwood grew up in Texas, the oldest of six, and studied visual art with a music minor at Brigham Young University. She is an author, multimedia artist, illustrator, comic creator, and designer with a love of stories. She has worked in publishing for the last six years. Rebecca lives in Utah with her husband, where she listens to audiobooks, cooks experimentally, has an interest in alternative health, and constantly has a new project in mind. Visit rebeccajgreenwood.com to experience more of her art and projects.